PRACTICAL REASON

PRACTICAL REASON

On the Theory of Action

PIERRE BOURDIEU

Stanford University Press
Stanford, California
1998

Stanford University Press
Stanford, California
© 1998 Polity Press this translation.
First published in France as *Raisons Pratiques,*
    © 1994 Éditions du Seuil.
This translation first published 1998 by Polity Press
    in association with Blackwell Publishers Ltd.
First published in the U.S.A. by Stanford University Press, 1998
Published with the assistance of the French Ministry of Culture
Printed in Great Britain
Cloth ISBN 0–8047–3362–7
Paper ISBN 0–8047–3363–5
LC 97–62102
This book is printed on acid-free paper.

CONTENTS

PREFACE

Situations where I have attempted to show foreign publics the universal validity of models constructed in relation to the specific case of France have perhaps allowed me to address, in these lectures, what I believe to be most essential in my work, that is, its most elementary and fundamental characteristics, which, no doubt through my own fault, often escape even the most well-intentioned readers and commentators.

First, it is a philosophy of science that one could call _relational_ in that it accords primacy to relations. Although characteristic of all modern science – if one believes authors as different as Cassirer and Bachelard – this philosophy is only rarely brought into play in the social sciences, undoubtedly because it is very directly opposed to the conventions of ordinary (or semi-scholarly) thought about the social world, which is more readily devoted to substantial "realities" such as individuals and groups than to the *objective relations* which one cannot show, but which must be captured, constructed and validated through scientific work.

Next, it is a philosophy of action designated at times as _dispositional_ which notes the potentialities inscribed in the body of agents and in the structure of the situations where they act or, more precisely, in the relations between them. This philosophy is condensed in a small number of fundamental concepts – habitus, field, capital – and its cornerstone is the two-way relationship between objective structures (those of social fields) and incorporated structures (those of the habitus). It is radically opposed to the anthropological presuppositions inscribed in the language which social

agents, and especially intellectuals, most commonly use to account
for practice (notably when, in the name of a narrow rationalism,
they consider irrational any action or representation which is not
generated by the explicitly posed reasons of an autonomous individual, fully conscious of his or her motivations). It is also opposed
to the more extreme theses of a certain structuralism by refusing to
reduce *agents*, which it considers to be eminently active and acting
(without necessarily doing so as subjects), to simple epiphenomena
of structure (which exposes it to seeming equally deficient to those
who hold one position or the other). This philosophy of action
asserts itself from the outset by breaking with a number of established notions which have been introduced in scholarly discourse
without examination ("subject," "motivation," "actor," "role,"
etc.) and with a whole series of socially powerful oppositions –
individual/society, individual/collective, conscious/unconscious,
interested/disinterested, objective/subjective, and so forth – which
seem to constitute ordinary thought.

I am aware that I have little chance of succeeding in truly transmitting, through the power of discourse alone, the principles of this
philosophy and the practical dispositions, the "métier," in which
they are embodied. Furthermore, I know that by designating them
as a philosophy, through a concession to ordinary usage, I risk
seeing them transformed into theoretical propositions, subject to
theoretical discussions, capable of again erecting obstacles to the
transmission of the constant and controlled ways of acting and
thinking which constitute a method. But I would like to hope that
I can at least contribute to dispelling the most tenacious misunder-
standings of my work, especially those which are often deliberately
kept alive by the indefatigable repetition of the same objections
without an object, the same absurd involuntary or voluntary reductions.[1] I am thinking, for example, of the accusations of "holism"
or "utilitarianism" and so many other categorical categorizations
engendered by the classificatory thought of *lectores* or by the reductive impatience of aspiring *auctores*.

It seems to me that the resistance of many intellectuals to sociological analysis, which is always suspected of crude reductionism, and which is found particularly odious when applied to their
own universe, is rooted in a sort of ill-placed (spiritualist) point
of honor which impedes them from accepting the realist representation of human action which is the first condition for scientific

knowledge of the social world. More precisely, it is grounded in an entirely inadequate idea of their own dignity as "subjects," which makes them see scientific analysis of practices as an attack on their "freedom" or their "disinterestedness."

It is true that sociological analysis hardly makes concessions to narcissism and that it carries out a radical rupture with the profoundly complaisant image of human existence defended by those who want, at all cost, to think of themselves as "the most irreplaceable of beings." But it is no less true that it is one of the most powerful instruments of self-knowledge as a social being, which is to say as a unique being. If such analysis questions the illusionary freedom granted by those who see in this form of self-knowledge a "descent into hell" and who periodically acclaim the last avatar of the latest fashion of the "sociology of freedom" – which a certain author was already defending under that name nearly 30 years ago – it also offers some of the most efficacious means of attaining the freedom from social determinisms which is possible only through knowledge of those very determinisms.

Note

1 The reference to these criticisms is, along with the need to recall the same principles on different occasions and to different publics, one of the reasons for the *repetitions* in this book, which I have chosen to maintain for the sake of clarity.

ACKNOWLEDGMENTS

Chapter 1 was originally presented as a lecture at the University of Todaï in October 1989. The English translation was previously published with the title "First Lecture. Social Space and Symbolic Space: Introduction to a Japanese Reading of *Distinction*" in *Poetics Today* 12:4 (Winter 1991), pp. 627–38. Copyright 1991, Porter Institute for Poetics and Semiotics, Tel Aviv University. Reprinted by permission of Duke University Press. It was translated by Gisele Sapiro and edited by Brian McHale.

The appendix to chapter 1 was originally a lecture delivered in East Berlin in October 1989. Part of it was previously published under the title "Supplement. *Distinction* Revisited: Introduction to an East German Reading" in *Poetics Today* 12:4 (Winter 1991), pp. 639–41. Copyright 1991, Porter Institute for Poetics and Semiotics, Tel Aviv University. Reprinted by permission of Duke University Press. It was translated by Gisele Sapiro and edited by Brian McHale. Randal Johnson translated the first four paragraphs not included in that version.

Chapter 2, which also originated as a lecture presented at the University of Todaï in October 1989, was previous published as "Second Lecture. The New Capital: Introduction to a Japanese reading of *State Nobility*," in *Poetics Today* 12:4 (Winter 1991), pp. 643–53. Copyright 1991, Porter Institute for Poetics and Semiotics, Tel Aviv University. Reprinted by permission of Duke University Press. It was translated by Gisele Sapiro and edited by Brian McHale.

The appendix to chapter 2 was originally a lecture delivered at the University of Wisconsin in April 1989. It was translated by Randal Johnson.

Chapter 3, originally a lecture delivered in Amsterdam in June 1991, was published in *Sociological Theory* 12:1 (Mar. 1994), pp. 1–18. It was translated by Loïc Wacquant and Samar Farage.

The appendix to chapter 3 was translated by Richard Nice and edited for this edition by Randal Johnson.

Chapter 4 is from a transcription of two courses of the Collège de France given at the Faculty of Anthropology and Sociology at the Université Lumière-Lyon II in December 1988. It was translated by Randal Johnson.

Chapter 5 is from a transcription of two courses of the Collège de France given at the Faculty of Anthropology and Sociology at the Université Lumière-Lyon II in February 1994. It was translated by Randal Johnson.

The appendix to chapter 5 was translated by Randal Johnson.

Chapter 6 was an address delivered at the conference "Geschmack, Strategien, praktiker Sinn" held at the Free University of Berlin in October 1989. It was translated by Loïc Wacquant.

The final chapter, "A Paradoxical Foundation of Ethics," was an address delivered at a conference in Locarno in May 1991, and appeared under the title "Towards a Policy of Morality in Politics" in William R. Shea and Antonio Spadafora (eds), *From the Twilight of Probability: Ethics and Politics*, Science History Publications, Canton, Mass., 1992, pp. 146–9. The translation was revised by Randal Johnson.

1

Social Space and Symbolic Space

I think that if I were Japanese I would dislike most of the things that non-Japanese people write about Japan. Over twenty years ago, at the time when I began to do research on French society, I recognized my irritation at American ethnologies of France in the criticism that Japanese sociologists, notably Hiroshi Miami and Tetsuro Watsuji, had levied against Ruth Benedict's famous book, *The Chrysanthemum and the Sword*. Thus, I shall not talk to you about the "Japanese sensibility," nor about the Japanese "mystery" or "miracle." I shall talk about France, a country I know fairly well, not because I was born there and speak its language, but because I have studied it a great deal. Does this mean that I shall confine myself to the particularity of a single society and shall not talk in any way about Japan? I do not think so. I think, on the contrary, that by presenting the model of social space and symbolic space that I constructed for the particular case of France, I shall still be speaking to you about Japan (just as, in other contexts, I would be speaking about Germany or the United States). For you to understand fully this discourse which concerns you and which might seem to you full of personal allusions when I speak about the French *homo academicus*, I would like to encourage you to go beyond a particularizing reading which, besides being an excellent defense mechanism against analysis, is the precise equivalent, on the reception side, of the curiosity for exotic particularism that has inspired so many works on Japan.

My work, and especially *Distinction*, is particularly exposed to such a reading. Its theoretical model is not embellished with all the marks by which one usually recognizes "grand theory," such as lack of any reference to some empirical reality. The notions of social space, symbolic space, or social class are never studied in and for themselves; rather, they are tested through research in which the theoretical and the empirical are inseparable and which mobilizes numerous methods of observation and measurement – quantitative and qualitative, statistical and ethnographic, macro-sociological and microsociological (all of which are meaningless oppositions) – for the purpose of studying an object well defined in space and time, that is, French society in the 1970s. The report of this research does not appear in the language to which certain sociologists, especially Americans, have accustomed us and whose appearance of universality is due only to the imprecision of a vocabulary hardly distinguishable from everyday usage (I shall mention only one example, the notion of "profession"). Thanks to a discursive montage which facilitates the juxtaposition of statistical tables, photographs, excerpts from interviews, facsimiles of documents, and the abstract language of analysis, this report makes the most abstract coexist with the most concrete, a photograph of the president of the Republic playing tennis or an interview with a baker with the most formal analysis of the generative and unifying power of the habitus.

My entire scientific enterprise is indeed based on the belief that the deepest logic of the social world can be grasped only if one plunges into the particularity of an empirical reality, historically located and dated, but with the objective of constructing it as a "special case of what is possible," as Bachelard puts it, that is, as an exemplary case in a finite world of possible configurations. Concretely, this means that an analysis of French social space in the 1970s is comparative history, which takes the present as its object, or comparative anthropology, which focuses on a particular cultural area: in both cases, the aim is to try to grasp the invariant, the structure in each variable observed.

I am convinced that, although it has all the appearance of ethnocentrism, an approach consisting of applying a model constructed according to this logic to another social world is without doubt more respectful of historical realities (and of people) and above all more fruitful in scientific terms than the interest in superficial features of the lover of exoticism who gives priority to picturesque differences (I am thinking, for instance, of what has been said and written, in the case of Japan, about the "culture of pleasure"). The researcher, both more modest and more ambitious than the collector of curiosities, seeks to apprehend the structures and mechanisms that are overlooked – although for different reasons – by the native and the foreigner alike, such as the principles of construction of social space or the mechanisms of reproduction of that space, and that the researcher seeks to represent in a model aspiring to a *universal validity*. In that way it is possible to register the real differences that separate both structures and dispositions (habitus), the principle of which must be sought not in the peculiarities of some national character – or "soul" – but in the particularities of different *collective histories*.

The Real is Relational

In this spirit I will presént the model I constructed in *Distinction*, first cautioning against a "substantialist" reading of analyses which intend to be structural or, better, relational (I refer here, without being able to go into detail, to the opposition suggested by Ernst Cassirer between "substantial concepts" and "functional or relational concepts"). The "substantialist" and naively realist reading considers each practice (playing golf, for example) or pattern of consumption (Chinese food, for instance) in and for itself, independently of the universe of substitutable practices, and conceives of the correspondence between social positions (or classes, thought of as substantial sets) and tastes or practices as a mechanical and direct relation. According to this logic, naive readers could consider as a refutation of the model the fact that, to take a perhaps facile example, Japanese or American intellectuals pretend to like French food, whereas French intellectuals like to go to Chinese or Japanese restaurants; or that the fancy shops of Tokyo or Fifth Avenue often have French names, whereas the fancy shops of the Faubourg Saint-Honoré display English names, such as "hairdresser." Another example which is, I believe, even more striking: in Japan, the rate of participation in general elections is highest among the least educated women of rural districts, whereas in France, as I demonstrated in an analysis of nonresponse to opinion polls, the rate of nonresponse – and of indifference to politics

– is especially high among women and among the least educated and the most economically and socially dispossessed. This is an example of a false difference that conceals a real one: the apathy associated with dispossession of the means of production of political opinions, which is expressed in France as simple absenteeism, translates, in the case of Japan, as a sort of apolitical participation. We should ask further what historical conditions (and here we should invoke the whole political history of Japan) have resulted in the fact that conservative parties in Japan have been able, through quite particular forms of clientelism, to benefit from the inclination toward unconditional delegation deriving from the conviction of not being in possession of the *statutory* and *technical* competence which is necessary for participation.

The substantialist mode of thought, which characterizes common sense – and racism – and which is inclined to treat the activities and preferences specific to certain individuals or groups in a society at a certain moment as if they were substantial properties, inscribed once and for all in a sort of biological or cultural *essence*, leads to the same kind of error, whether one is comparing different societies or successive periods in the same society. Some would thus consider the fact that, for example, tennis or even golf is not nowadays as exclusively associated with dominant positions as in the past, or that the noble sports, such as riding or fencing (or, in Japan, the martial arts), are no longer specific to nobility as they originally were, as a refutation of the proposed model, which figure 1, presenting the correspondence between the space of constructed classes and the space of practices, captures in a visual and synoptic way.[1] An initially aristocratic practice can be given up by the aristocracy – and this occurs quite frequently – when it is adopted by a growing fraction of the bourgeoisie or petit-bourgeoisie, or even the lower classes (this is what happened in France to boxing, which was enthusiastically practiced by aristocrats at the end of the nineteenth century). Conversely, an initially lower-class practice can sometimes be taken up by nobles. In short, one has to avoid turning into necessary and intrinsic properties of some group (nobility, samurai, as well as workers or employees) the properties which belong to this group at a given moment in time because of its position in a determinate social space and in a determinate state of the *supply* of possible goods and practices. Thus, at every moment of each society, one has to

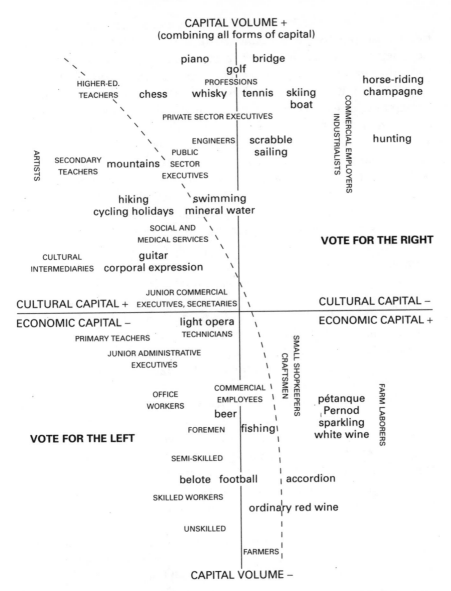

Figure 1 The space of social positions and the space of lifestyles (the dotted line indicates probable orientation toward the right or left)

deal with a set of social positions which is bound by a relation of homology to a set of activities (the practice of golf or piano) or of goods (a second home or an old master painting) that are themselves characterized relationally.

This formula, which might seem abstract and obscure, states the first conditions for an adequate reading of the analysis of the relation between *social positions* (a relational concept), *dispositions* (or habitus), and *position-takings* (*prises de position*), that is, the "choices" made by the social agents in the most diverse domains of practice, in food or sport, music or politics, and so forth. It is a reminder that comparison is possible only from *system to system*, and that the search for direct equivalences between features grasped in isolation, whether, appearing at first sight different, they prove to be "functionally" or technically equivalent (like Pernod and *shôchû* or saké) or nominally identical (the practice of golf in France and Japan, for instance), risks unduly identifying structurally different properties or wrongly distinguishing structurally identical properties. The very title *Distinction* serves as a reminder that what is commonly called distinction, that is, a certain quality of bearing and manners, most often considered innate (one speaks of *distinction naturelle*, "natural refinement"), is nothing other than *difference*, a gap, a distinctive feature, in short, a *relational* property existing only in and through its relation with other properties.

This idea of difference, or a gap, is at the basis of the very notion of *space*, that is, a set of distinct and coexisting positions which are exterior to one another and which are defined in relation to one another through their *mutual exteriority* and their relations of proximity, vicinity, or distance, as well as through relations of order, such as above, below, and *between*. Certain properties of members of the petit-bourgeoisie can, for example, be deduced from the fact that they occupy an intermediate position between two extreme positions, without being objectively identifiable and subjectively identified either with one or the other position.

Social space is constructed in such a way that agents or groups are distributed in it according to their position in statistical distributions based on the *two principles of differentiation* which, in the most advanced societies, such as the United States, Japan, or France, are undoubtedly the most efficient: economic capital and cultural capital. It follows that all agents are located in this space in such a way that the closer they are to one another in those two dimensions, the more they have in common; and the more remote they are from one another, the less they have in common. Spatial distances on paper are equivalent to social distances. More precisely, as expressed in the diagram in *Distinction* in which I tried to represent social space (figure 1), agents are distributed in the first dimension according to the overall volume of the different kinds of capital they possess, and in the second dimension according to the structure of their capital, that is, according to the relative weight of the different kinds of capital, economic and cultural, in the total volume of their capital.

Thus, in the first dimension, which is undoubtedly the most important, the holders of a great volume of overall capital, such as industrial employers, members of liberal professions, and university professors are opposed, in the mass, to those who are most deprived of economic and cultural capital, such as unskilled workers. But from another point of view, that is, from the point of view of the relative weight of economic capital and cultural capital in their patrimony, professors (relatively wealthier in cultural capital than in economic capital) are strongly opposed to industrial employers (relatively wealthier in economic capital than in cultural capital), and this is no doubt as true in Japan as in France (although it remains to be verified).

The second opposition, like the first, is the source of differences in dispositions and, therefore, in position-takings. This is the case of the opposition between intellectuals and industrial employers or, on a lower level of the social hierarchy, between primary school teachers and small merchants, which, in postwar France and Japan alike, translates, in politics, into an opposition between left and right (as is suggested in the diagram, the probability of leaning politically toward the right or the left depends at least as much on the position in the horizontal dimension as on the position in the vertical dimension, that is, on the relative weight of cultural capital and economic capital in the volume of capital possessed at least as much as on the volume itself).

In a more general sense, the space of social positions is retranslated into a space of position-takings through the mediation of the space of dispositions (or habitus). In other words, the system of differential deviations which defines the different positions in the two major dimensions of social space corresponds to the system of differential deviations in agents' properties (or in the properties of constructed classes of agents), that is, in their practices and in the goods they possess. To each class of positions there corresponds a class of habitus (or *tastes*) produced by the social conditioning associated with the corresponding condition and, through the mediation of the habitus and its generative capability, a systematic set of goods and properties, which are united by an affinity of style.

One of the functions of the notion of habitus is to account for the unity of style, which unites the practices and goods of a single agent or a class of agents (this is what writers such as Balzac or Flaubert have so finely expressed through their descriptions of settings – such as the Pension Vauquer in *Le Père Goriot* or the elegant dishes and drinks consumed in the homes of different protagonists of *L'Éducation sentimentale* – which are at the same time descriptions of the characters who live in them). The habitus is this generative and unifying principle which retranslates the intrinsic and relational characteristics of a position into a unitary lifestyle, that is, a unitary set of choices of persons, goods, practices.

Like the positions of which they are the product, habitus are differentiated, but they are also differentiating. Being distinct and distinguished, they are also distinction operators, implementing different principles of differentiation or using differently the common principles of differentiation.

Habitus are generative principles of distinct and distinctive practices – what the worker eats, and especially the way he eats it, the sport he practices and the way he practices it, his political opinions and the way he expresses them are systematically different from the industrial owner's corresponding activities. But habitus are also classificatory schemes, principles of classification, principles of vision and division, different tastes. They make distinctions between what is good and what is bad, between what is right and what is wrong, between what is distinguished and what is vulgar, and so forth, but the distinctions are not identical. Thus, for instance, the same behavior or even the same good can appear distinguished to one person, pretentious to someone else, and cheap or showy to yet another.

But the essential point is that, when perceived through these social categories of perception, these principles of vision and division, the differences in practices, in the goods possessed, or in the opinions expressed become symbolic differences and constitute a veritable *language*. Differences associated with different positions, that is, goods, practices, and especially *manners*, function, in each society, in the same way as differences which constitute symbolic systems, such as the set of phonemes of a language or the set of distinctive features and of differential *"écarts"* that constitute a mythical system, that is, as *distinctive signs*.

Here I open a parenthesis in order to dispel a frequent, yet disastrous, misunderstanding about the title *Distinction*, which has led some to believe that the entire book was limited to saying that the driving force of all human behavior was the search for distinction. This does not make sense and, moreover, it would not be anything new if one thinks, for example, of Veblen and his notion of conspicuous consumption. In fact, the main idea is that to exist within a social space, to occupy a point or to be an individual within a social space, is to differ, to be different. According to Benveniste's formula regarding language, "to be distinctive, to be significant, is the same thing," significant being opposed to insignificant, or to different meanings. More precisely – Benveniste's formulation is a little too quick . . . – a difference, a distinctive property, white or black skin, slenderness or stoutness, Volvo or VW Beetle, red wine or champagne, Pernod or scotch, golf or soccer, piano or accordion, bridge or *belote* (I proceed with oppositions, because things tend to operate in this fashion most of the time, although the situation is more complicated than this), only becomes a visible, perceptible, non-indifferent, socially *pertinent* difference if it is perceived by someone who is capable of *making the distinction* – because, being inscribed in the space in question, he or she is not *indifferent* and is endowed with categories of perception, with classificatory schemata, with a certain *taste*, which permits her to make differences, to discern, to distinguish – between a color print and a painting or between Van Gogh and Gauguin. Difference becomes a sign and a sign of distinction (or vulgarity) only if a principle of vision and division is applied to it which, being the product of the incorporation of the structure of objective differences (for example, the structure of the distribution in the social space of the piano or the accordion or those who prefer one or the other), is present among all the agents, piano owners or accordion lovers, and structures the perceptions of owners or lovers of pianos or accordions (there was a need to spell out this analysis of the logic – that of symbolic violence – according to which dominated lifestyles are almost always perceived, even by those who live them, from the destructive and reductive point of view of the dominant aesthetic).

The Logic of Classes

To construct social space, this invisible reality that cannot be shown but which organizes agents' practices and representations, is at the same time to create the possibility of constructing *theoretical classes* that are as homogeneous as possible from the point of view of the two major determinants of practices and of all their attendant properties. The principle of classification thus put into play is genuinely *explanatory*. It is not content with describing the set of classified realities, but rather, like the good taxonomies of the natural sciences, it fixes on determinant properties which, unlike the apparent differences of bad classifications, allow for the prediction of the other properties and which distinguish and bring together agents who are as similar to each other as possible and as different as possible from members of other classes, whether adjacent or remote.

But the very validity of the classification risks encouraging a perception of theoretical classes, which are fictitious regroupings existing only *on paper*, through an intellectual decision by the researcher, as *real* classes, real groups, that are constituted as such in reality. The danger is all the greater as the research makes it appear that the divisions drawn in *Distinction* do indeed correspond to real differences in the most different, and even the most unexpected, domains of practice. Thus, to take the example of a curious property, the distribution of the dog and cat owners is organized according to the model: commercial employers (on the right in figure 1) tend to prefer dogs, intellectuals (on the left in figure 1) tend to prefer cats.

The model thus defines distances that are *predictive* of encounters, affinities, sympathies, or even desires. Concretely, this means that people located at the top of the space have little chance of marrying people located toward the bottom, first because they have little chance of physically meeting them (except in what are called "bad places," that is, at the cost of a transgression of the social limits which reflect spatial distances); secondly because, if they do accidentally meet them on some occasion, they will not get on together, will not really understand each other, will not appeal to one another. On the other hand, proximity in social space predisposes to closer relations: people who are inscribed in a restricted sector of the space will be both closer (in their properties and in their dispositions, *their tastes*) and more disposed to get closer, as well as being easier to bring together, to mobilize. *But this does not mean that they constitute a class in Marx's sense, that is, a group which is mobilized for common purposes, and especially against another class.*

The theoretical classes that I construct are, more than any other theoretical divisions (more, for example, than divisions according to sex, ethnicity, and so on), predisposed to become classes in the Marxist sense of the term. If I am a political leader and I propose creating one big party bringing together both industrial employers and workers, I have little chance of success, since these groups are very distant in social space; in a certain conjuncture, in a national crisis, on the bases of nationalism or chauvinism, it will be possible for them to draw closer, but this solidarity will still be rather superficial and very provisional. This does not mean that, inversely, proximity in social space automatically engenders unity. It defines an objective potentiality of unity or, to speak like Leibniz, a "claim to exist" as a group, a *probable class*. Marxist theory makes a mistake quite similar to the one Kant denounced in the ontological argument or to the one for which Marx criticized Hegel: it makes a "death-defying leap" from existence in theory to existence in practice, or, as Marx puts it, "from the things of logic to the logic of things."

Marx, who more than any other theoretician exerted the *theory effect* – the properly political effect that consists in making tangible (*theorein*) a "reality" that cannot entirely exist insofar as it remains unknown and unrecognized – paradoxically failed to take this effect into account in his own theory... One moves from class-on-paper to the "real" class only at the price of a political work of mobilization. The "real" class, if it has ever "really" existed, is nothing but the realized class, that is, the mobilized class, a result of the *struggle of classifications*, which is a properly symbolic (and political) struggle to impose a vision of the social world, or, better, a way to construct that world, in perception and in reality, and to construct classes in accordance with which this social world can be divided.

The very existence of classes, as everyone knows from his or her own experience, is a stake in a struggle. And this fact undoubtedly constitutes the major obstacle to a scientific knowledge of the social world and to the resolution (for *there is one*...)

of the problem of social classes. Denying the existence of classes, as the conservative tradition has persisted in doing for reasons not all of which are absurd (and all research done in good faith encounters them along the way), means in the final analysis denying the existence of differences and of principles of differentiation. This is just what those who pretend that nowadays the American, Japanese, and French societies are each nothing but an enormous "middle class" do, although in a more paradoxical way, since those who believe this nevertheless preserve the term "class" (according to a survey, 80 percent of the Japanese say they belong to the "middle class"). This position is, of course, unsustainable. All my work shows that in a country said to be on the way to becoming homogenized, democratized, and so on, difference is everywhere. And in the United States, every day some new piece of research appears showing diversity where one *expected to see* homogeneity, conflict where one expected to see consensus, reproduction and conservation where one expected to see mobility. Thus, *difference* (which I express in describing social *space*) exists and persists. But does this mean that we must accept or affirm the existence of classes? No. Social classes do not exist (even if political work, armed with Marx's theory, had in some cases contributed to making them at least exist through instances of mobilization and proxies). What exists is a social space, a space of differences, in which classes exist in some sense in a state of virtuality, not as something given but as *something to be done*.

Nevertheless, if the social world, with its divisions, is something that social agents have to do, to construct, individually and especially *collectively*, in cooperation and conflict, these constructions still do not take place in a social void, as certain ethnomethodologists seem to believe. The position occupied in social space, that is, in the structure of the distribution of different kinds of capital, which are also weapons, commands the representations of this space and the position-takings in the struggles to conserve or transform it.

To summarize the intricate relation between objective structures and subjective constructions, which is located beyond the usual alternatives of objectivism and subjectivism, of structuralism and constructivism, and even of materialism and idealism, I usually quote, with a little distortion, a famous formula of Pascal's: "The world comprehends me and swallows me like a point, but I comprehend it." The social world embraces me like a point. But this point is a *point of view*, the principle of a view adopted from a point located in social space, a *perspective* which is defined, in its form and contents, by the objective position from which it is adopted. The social space is indeed the first and last reality, since it still commands the representations that the social agents can have of it.

I am coming to the end of what has been a kind of introduction to the reading of *Distinction*, in which I have undertaken to state the principles of a relational, structural reading that is capable of developing the full import of the model I propose. A relational but also a *generative* reading. By this I mean that I hope my readers will try to apply the model in this other "particular case of the possible," that is, Japanese society, that they will try to construct the Japanese social space and symbolic space, to define the basic principles of objective differentiation (I think they are the same, but one should verify whether, for instance, they do not have different relative weights – I do not think so, given the exceptional importance which is traditionally attributed to education in Japan) and especially the principles of distinction, the specific distinctive signs in the domains of sport, food, drink, and so on, the relevant features which make significant differences in the different symbolic subspaces. This is, in my opinion, the condition for a *comparativism of the essential* that I called for at the beginning and, at the same time, for the universal knowledge of the invariants and variations that sociology can and must produce.

As for me, I shall undertake in my next lecture to say what the mechanisms are which, in France as in Japan and all other advanced countries, guarantee the reproduction of social space and symbolic space, without ignoring the contradictions and conflicts that can be at the basis of their transformation.

Notes

This is the text of a lecture presented at the University of Todaï in October 1989.

1 Cf. Pierre Bourdieu, *Distinction: a Social Critique of the Judgement of Taste*, trans. Richard Nice (Cambridge: Harvard University Press, 1984), pp. 128–9; figure 1 is a simplified version of the one appearing there.

APPENDIX

The "Soviet" Variant and Political Capital

I know that a number of you have undertaken a thorough reading of *Distinction*. I would like to go over the book with you again, attempting to respond to the question that you have no doubt asked yourselves: is the model proposed in that book valid beyond the particular case of France? Can it also be applied to the case of the German Democratic Republic and, if so, under what conditions?

If one wants to demonstrate that it is a universal model, which permits one to account for historical variations at the cost of certain transformations of variables that must be taken into account universally (or, at least, in differentiated societies) in order to explain the differentiation that constitutes social space, it is first necessary to break with the propensity toward substantialist and naively realist thought which, instead of focusing on relations, limits itself to the phenomenal realities in which they are manifested. Such thought impedes one from recognizing the same opposition between the dominant and the dominated when, in different countries, or at different moments in the same country, it is inscribed in phenomenally different practices. For example, the practice of tennis, which until recently (and still during the period when the survey that served as the basis of *Distinction* was undertaken) was reserved, at least in France, for the occupants of the highest positions in the social space, has become much more common, although differences continue to exist, but in terms of the places, moments, and forms of its practice. Such examples could be multiplied, borrowing from all universes of practice or consumption.

It is thus necessary to construct social space as a structure of differentiated positions, defined in each case by the place they occupy in the distribution of a particular kind of capital. Social classes, according to this logic, are only logical, determined classes in theory and, if I may say, on paper, through the delimitation of a (relatively) homogeneous set of agents occupying an identical position in social space. They can only become mobilized and active classes, in the sense of the Marxist tradition, at the cost of a properly political work of construction, indeed of fabrication – in E. P. Thompson's sense when he speaks of *The Making of the English Working Class*[1] – in which success can be facilitated, but not determined, by belonging to the same sociological class.

In order to construct social space, in the case of France it was necessary and sufficient to consider the different kinds of capital whose distribution determines the structure of that social space. Since in France economic capital and cultural capital have a very important weight, social space is organized according to three fundamental dimensions: in the first dimension, agents are distributed according to the overall volume of the capital of all kinds that they possess; in the second, according to the structure of that capital, that is, according to the relative weight of economic capital and cultural capital in their patrimony; in the third, according to the evolution over time of the volume and structure of their capital. Due to the correspondence established between the space of positions occupied in the social space and the space of the dispositions (or habitus) of their occupants and also, through the mediation of the latter, the space of position-takings, the model functions as an adequate principle of classification. The classes that can be produced by demarcating regions of the social space bring together agents as homogeneous as possible, not only from the point of view of their conditions of existence, but also from the point of view of their cultural practices, their patterns of consumption, their public opinions, and so forth.

To respond to the question raised at the outset and verify whether the model proposed in *Distinction* can be applied to the case of the GDR, it is necessary to investigate what principles of differentiation are characteristic of this society (which amounts to admitting, contrary to the myth of the "classless society," that is, of a society without differences, that such principles do indeed exist, as the protest movements currently active in the country conspicuously attest); or, to put it more simply, to determine whether, in the case of the GDR, one rediscovers all (and only) the same principles of differentiation, bearing the same relative weights, as those encountered in France. Right from the beginning one sees that among the major differences between the two spaces and the respective principles of differentiation defining them is the fact that economic capital – private possession of the means of production – is *officially* (and, for the most part, in actual fact) out of bounds in the GDR (even if a form of access to the advantages that are elsewhere furnished by economic capital can be secured in other ways). The relative weight of cultural capital (which can be assumed to be highly valued in the German tradition, as in the French or Japanese) is proportionally increased.

It goes without saying, however, that, whatever an official meritocratic ideology may want people to believe, not all the differences in opportunities for appropriating scarce goods and services can reasonably be related to differences in possession of cultural and educational capital. It is thus necessary to hypothesize another principle of differentiation, another kind of capital, the unequal distribution of which is the source of the observable differences in patterns of consumption and lifestyles. I am thinking here of what could be called *political capital*, which guarantees its holders a form of private appropriation of goods and public services (residences, cars, hospitals, schools, and so on). This patrimonialization of collective resources can also be observed when, as in the case of Scandinavian countries, a social-democratic "elite" has been in power for several generations; one then sees how the political type of social capital, acquired through the apparatus of the trade unions and the Labour Party, is transmitted through networks of family relations, leading to the constitution of true political dynasties. The regimes that are properly called "Soviet" (rather than communist) have carried to the limit this tendency toward *private appropriation of public goods and services* (which is also evident, although less intensively so, in French socialism).

When other forms of accumulation are more or less completely controlled, political capital becomes the primordial principle of differentiation, and the members of the political "nomenklatura" have hardly any competitors in the struggle for the dominant principle of domination which takes place in the field of power, other than the holders of academic capital. Indeed, everything leads us to suppose that the recent changes in Russia and elsewhere have their source in rivalries between the holders of political capital, of the first and especially the second generations, and the holders of academic capital, technocrats and especially researchers or intellectuals, who themselves come partly from the political nomenklatura.

The introduction of an index of a specifically political capital of the Soviet type – an index that would have to be elaborated with some care, taking into account not only positions in the hierarchy of political apparatuses (in the first place, that of the Communist Party itself), but also the seniority of each agent and of his lineage among the political dynasties – would no doubt enable us to construct a representation of social space capable of accounting for the distribution of powers and privileges, as well as of lifestyles. But, here again, in order to account for the particularity of the German case, notably the somewhat gray and uniform tone of its forms of public sociability, one should take into account not the Puritan tradition so much as the fact that the categories capable of furnishing cultural models have been depleted by emigration and especially by the political and moral control which, because of the egalitarian pretensions of the regime, is exerted on external expressions of difference.

One could ask, by way of verification, to what extent the model of social space thus obtained would be able to account, at least roughly, for the conflicts arising in the GDR today. There is no doubt that, as I have suggested, the holders of academic capital are those most inclined to be impatient and to revolt against the privileges of the holders of political capital, and they are also those best able to turn against the nomenklatura the egalitarian or meritocratic tenets that form the basis of its claims to legitimacy. But one might well wonder whether the intellectuals who dream of creating a "real socialism" in opposition to the caricature produced and imposed by apparatchiks (especially those apparatchiks who, nonentities outside the apparatus, are prepared to give their all for an apparatus that has given them all) will succeed in establishing a real and durable alliance with the dominated, particularly the manual workers, who cannot help but be susceptible to the "demonstration effect" of common or garden capitalism, that is, the capitalism of the refrigerator, the washing machine, and the Volkswagen; or even with the minor state bureaucrats who cannot find in the shabby security afforded by a third-rate welfare state (and purchased at the cost of conspicuous deprivations) sufficient grounds for refusing the immediate satisfactions promised by a liberal economy limited by state intervention and the moderating influence of social movements – even if those satisfactions are fraught with risks (notably that of unemployment).

Appendix Notes

This is the text of a lecture delivered in East Berlin, October 25, 1989.

1 Edward P. Thompson, *The Making of the English Working Class* (New York: Pantheon, 1964).

2

The New Capital

oday I would like to speak about the extremely complex mechanisms through which the school institution *contributes* (I insist on this word) to the reproduction of the distribution of cultural capital and, consequently, of the structure of social space. Corresponding to the two basic dimensions of this space, which I mentioned yesterday, are two sets of different mechanisms of reproduction, the combination of which defines the *mode of reproduction* and ensures that capital finds its way to capital and that the social structure tends to perpetuate itself (not without undergoing more or less important deformations). The reproduction of the structure of the distribution of cultural capital is achieved in the relation between familial strategies and the specific logic of the school institution.

Families are *corporate bodies* animated by a kind of *conatus*, in Spinoza's sense, that is, a tendency to perpetuate their social being, with all its powers and privileges, which is at the basis of *reproduction strategies*: fertility strategies, matrimonial strategies, successional strategies, economic strategies, and last but not least, educational strategies. Families invest all the more in school education (in transmission time, in help of all kinds, and in some cases, as today in Japan, in money, as with the Juku and the Yobi-ko[1]) as their cultural capital is more important and as the relative weight of their cultural capital in relation to their economic capital is greater – and also as the other reproduction strategies (especially successional strategies, which aim at the direct transmission of economic capital) are less effective or relatively less profitable (as has been the case in Japan since the Second World War and, to a lesser degree, in France).

This model, which may seem very abstract, allows us to understand the growing interest that families and especially privileged families, including the families of intellectuals, teachers, or members of liberal professions, have in education in all advanced countries and, undoubtedly, in Japan more than anywhere else. It also allows us to understand how the highest school institutions, those which give access to the highest social positions, become increasingly monopolized by the children of privileged categories, which is as true in Japan and the United States as it is in France. More broadly, this model enables us to understand not only how advanced societies perpetuate themselves, but also how they change under the effect of the specific contradictions of the scholastic mode of reproduction.

The School: Maxwell's Demon?

For an overview of the functioning of the mechanism of scholastic reproduction, one might evoke, by way of first approximation, the image that physicist James Clerk Maxwell used in explaining how the Second Law of Thermodynamics could be suspended. Maxwell imagined a demon who sorts the moving particles passing before him, some being warmer, therefore faster moving, others cooler, therefore slower moving; the demon sends the fastest particles into one container, whose temperature rises, and the slowest into another container, whose temperature falls. He thereby maintains difference and order, which would otherwise tend to be annihilated. The educational system acts like Maxwell's demon: at the cost of the energy which is necessary for carrying out the sorting operation, it maintains the preexisting order, that is, the gap between pupils endowed with unequal amounts of cultural capital. More precisely, by a series of selection operations, the system separates the holders of inherited cultural capital from those who lack it. Differences of aptitude being inseparable from social differences according to inherited capital, the system thus tends to maintain preexisting social differences.

Moreover, it produces two effects which can be accounted for only if we give up the (dangerous) language of mechanism. In establishing a split between the students of the prestigious Grandes

Écoles and regular university students, the school institution institutes *social borders* analogous to those which formerly separated nobility from gentry and gentry from common people. This separation is marked, first of all, in the very conditions of life, in the opposition between the reclusive life of boarding schools, on the one hand, and the free life of the regular university student, on the other; then in the contents and especially the organization of the course of preparatory study toward the competitive examinations, with, on the one hand, very strict supervision and highly scholastic forms of apprenticeship, especially a high-pressure, competitive atmosphere which inspires submissiveness and presents a conspicuous analogue to the business world, and, on the other hand, "student life," closely related to the tradition of bohemian life and requiring much less in the way of discipline and constraint, even during the time devoted to work. By means of the competitive examination and the ordeal of preparing for it, as well as through the ritual cut-off – a true magical threshold separating the last candidate to have passed from the first to have failed, instituting a difference in kind indicated by the right to bear a *name*, a *title* – the school institution performs a truly magical operation, the paradigm of which is the separation between the sacred and the profane according to Durkheim's analysis.

The act of scholastic classification is always, but especially in this case, an act of *ordination*, in the double sense the word has in French. It institutes a social difference of rank, a *permanent relation of order*: the elect are marked, for their whole lives, by their affiliation ("old boys" of such-and-such an institution); they are members of an *order*, in the medieval sense of the word, and of a noble order, that is, a clearly delimited set (one either belongs or one doesn't) of people who are separated from the common run of mortals by a difference of essence and, therefore, legitimately licensed to dominate. This is why the separation achieved by school is also an act of ordination in the sense of *consecration*, enthronement in a sacred category, a nobility.

Familiarity prevents us from seeing everything that is concealed in the apparently purely technical acts achieved by the school institution. Thus, the Weberian analysis of a certificate as *Bildungspatent* and of the examination as a process of rational selection, without being strictly false, is nevertheless *partial*. Indeed, it overlooks the magical aspect of school operations, which also fulfill functions of *rationalization*, but not in the Weberian sense. Tests or competitive examinations *justify in reason* divisions that do not necessarily stem from reason, and the titles which sanction their results present *certificates* of social competence, not unlike titles of nobility, as guarantees of technical competence. In all advanced societies, in France, the United States, or Japan, social success depends very strictly on an initial act of *nomination* (the assigning of a name, usually the name of an educational institution, Todaï University or Harvard University or École Polytechnique) which consecrates scholastically a preexisting social difference.

The presentation of diplomas, often the occasion for solemn ceremonies, is quite comparable with the dubbing of a knight. The conspicuously (all too conspicuously) technical function of formation, of transmission of a technical competence and selection of the most technically competent, conceals a social function, that is, the consecration of the statutory bearers of social competence, of the right to rule. We thus have, in Japan as well as in France, a *hereditary scholastic nobility* (the *nisei*, or second generation, as it is called in Japan) of leaders of industry, great doctors, higher civil servants, and even political leaders, and this scholastic nobility includes an important segment of the heirs of the old bloodline nobility who have *converted* their noble titles into academic titles.

Thus, the school institution, once thought capable of introducing a form of meritocracy by privileging individual aptitudes over hereditary privileges, actually tends to establish, through the hidden linkage between scholastic aptitude and cultural heritage, a veritable *state nobility*, whose authority and legitimacy are guaranteed by the academic title. A review of history suffices to reveal that the reign of this specific nobility, aligned with the state, is the result of a long process: state nobility, in France and no doubt in Japan as well, is a corporate body which, created in the course of the state's creation, had indeed to create the state in order to create itself as holder of a legitimate monopoly on state power. The state nobility is the inheritor of what is called in France "*noblesse de robe*" (nobility recruited from the legal profession), which is distinguished from the "*noblesse d'épée*," or nobility of the sword (with which it nonetheless increasingly allied itself over time through marriage), in that it owes its status to cultural capital, essentially of a juridical type.

I cannot rehearse here the whole historical analysis outlined in the last chapter of *The State Nobility*,[2] based on the works, which are seldom brought together, of historians of education, historians of the state, and historians of ideas. This analysis could serve as the basis for a systematic comparison between this process and the one (which I believe to be quite similar, despite all the apparent differences) that led the samurai, one segment of whom had already in the course of the seventeenth century been transformed into a literate bureaucracy, to promote, in the second half of the nineteenth century, a modern state based on a body of bureaucrats in whom noble origin and a strong scholastic culture were combined, a body anxious to affirm its independence in and through a cult of the national state and characterized by an aristocratic sense of superiority relative to industrialists and merchants, let alone politicians.

To return to the French case, one might observe that the invention of the state and, especially, of the ideas of the "public," "common welfare," and "public service" which are at its heart, are inseparable from the invention of the institutions that ground the power of the state nobility and its reproduction. Thus, for instance, the stages of development of the school institution, and particularly the emergence in the eighteenth century of institutions of a new type, the "colleges," mixing certain segments of the aristocracy and of the bourgeoisie of the robe in boarding schools that anticipated the present system of Grandes Écoles, coincide with the stages of development of the state bureaucracy (and secondarily, at least in the sixteenth century, the Church bureaucracy). The autonomization of the bureaucratic field and the multiplication of positions independent of the established temporal and spiritual powers are accompanied by the development of a bourgeoisie of the robe and a *noblesse de robe*, whose interests are strongly bound up with those of the school institution, notably in the realm of reproduction. In its art of living, which accords a large place to cultural practices, as well as in its system of values, this kind of *Bildungsburgertum*, as the Germans say, defines itself as opposed, on the one hand, to the clergy and, on the other, to the *noblesse d'épée*, criticizing its ideology of birth in the name of merit and of what will later come to be called competence. Finally, the modern ideology of public service, of common welfare and commonweal, in short what has been called the "civic humanism of the civil servants," which would inspire the French Revolution (notably through the Girondist lawyers), was invented collectively (although the history of ideas prefers to credit individuals) by the classes of the robe.

Thus, one can see how the new class, the power and authority of which rests on the new cultural capital, has to elevate its particular interests to a superior degree of universalization and invent a version of the ideology of public service and of meritocracy that could be considered "progressive" (compared with the aristocratic variant that German and Japanese civil servants would later invent) in order to prevail in its struggles with the other dominant fractions, the *noblesse d'épée* and the industrial and mercantile bourgeoisie. Demanding power in the name of the universal, the nobility and bourgeoisie of the robe promote the objectification and therefore the historical efficacy of the universal; they cannot make use of the state they claim to serve unless they also serve, however slightly, the universal values with which they identify it.

Art or Money?

I could end my argument here, but I would like to reexamine briefly the image of Maxwell's demon which I used earlier to make a point, but which, like all metaphors borrowed from physics and in particular from thermodynamics, implies a completely false philosophy of action and a conservative vision of the social world (as evidenced by the conscious or unconscious use made of it by those, such as Heidegger, who criticize "leveling" and the gradual annihilation of "authentic" differences in the dull, flat banality of the "average"). As a matter of fact, social agents, students choosing an educational track or discipline, families choosing an institution for their children, and so on, are not particles subject to mechanical forces and acting under the constraint of *causes*; nor are they conscious and knowing subjects acting with full knowledge of the facts, as the champions of *rational action theory* believe. (I could show, if I had enough time, that these two philosophies, which seem diametrically opposed, are in fact similar; for, granted perfect knowledge of all the ins and outs of the question, all its causes and effects, and granted a completely logical choice, one is at a loss to know wherein such a "choice" would differ from pure and simple submission to outside forces or where, consequently, there would be any "choice" in the matter at all.)

In fact, "subjects" are active and knowing agents endowed with a *practical sense*, that is, an acquired system of preferences, of principles of vision and division (what is usually called taste), and also a system of durable cognitive structures (which are essentially the product of the internalization of objective structures) and of schemes of action which orient the perception of the situation and the appropriate response. The habitus is this kind of practical sense for what is to be done in a given situation – what is called in sport a "feel" for the game, that is, the art of *anticipating* the future of the game, which is inscribed in the present state of play. To take an example from the realm of education, the "feel" for the game becomes increasingly necessary as the educational tracks (as is the case in France as well as Japan) become diversified and confused (how to choose between a famous but declining institution and a rising "second-tier" school?). It is difficult to anticipate fluctuations on the stock exchange of scholastic value, and those who have the benefit, through family, parents, brothers, sisters, acquaintances, and so on, of information about the formation circuits and their actual or potential differential profit can make better educational investments and earn maximum returns on their cultural capital. This is one of the mediations through which scholastic – and social – success are linked to social origin.

In other words, the "particles" which move toward the "demon" carry in them, that is, in their habitus, the law of their direction and of their movement, the principle of their "vocation" which directs them toward a specific school, university, or discipline. I have made a lengthy analysis of how the relative weight of economic and cultural capital (what I call the structure of capital) in the capital of teenagers (or of their families) is retranslated into a system of preferences which induce them either to privilege art over money, cultural things over the business of power, and so on, or the opposite; how this structure of capital, through the system of preferences it produces, motivates them to direct themselves in their educational and social choices toward one or the other pole of the field of power, the intellectual pole or the business pole, and to adopt the corresponding practices and opinions. (Thus one can understand what seems so self-evident because we are so used to it, for instance, that the students of the École Normale, the future professors or intellectuals, have a greater tendency to present themselves as left-wing and read intellectual reviews, whereas HEC[3] students have a greater tendency to present themselves as right-wing, to practice sport intensively, and so on.)

Likewise, in place of the metaphorical demon, there are many "demons," among them the thousands of professors who apply to the students categories of perception and appreciation which are structured according to the same principles (I cannot develop here the analysis I have made of the categories of professorial understanding, the paired adjectives such as "bright/dull," in terms of which the master judges the productions of the students and all their manners, their ways of being and doing). In other words, the action of the educational system results from the more or less orchestrated actions of thousands of small versions of Maxwell's demon who, by their well-ordered choices aligned with the objective order (the structuring structures are, let me repeat, structured structures), tend to reproduce this order without either knowing they are doing so or wanting to do so.

But the demon metaphor is dangerous again, because it favors the conspiratorial fantasy which so often haunts critical thinking, that is, the idea of a malevolent will which is responsible for everything that occurs in the social world, for better and especially for worse. What we are justified in describing as a *mechanism*, in the interests of making a point, is sometimes experienced as a kind of *infernal engine* (we often speak of the "hell of success"), as though agents were no more than tragic cogs in a machine that is exterior and superior to them all. The reason for this is that each agent is somehow constrained, in order to exist, to participate in a game which requires great efforts and great sacrifices.

And I think that, in fact, the social order guaranteed in part by the scholastic mode of reproduction today subjects even those who profit from it to a degree of tension which is quite comparable to what court society, as described by Norbert Elias, imposed on the very agents who had the extraordinary privilege to belong to it.

In the last analysis this compelling struggle for ever-threatened power and prestige was the dominant factor that condemned all those involved to enact the burdensome ceremonies. No single

person within the figuration was able to initiate a reform of the tradition. Every slightest attempt to reform, to change the precarious
structure of tensions, inevitably entailed an upheaval, a reduction
or even abolition of the rights of certain individuals and families.
To jeopardize such privileges was, to the ruling class of this society,
a kind of taboo. The attempt would be opposed by broad sections
of the privileged who feared, perhaps not without justification,
that the whole system of rule that gave them privilege would be
threatened or would collapse if the slightest detail of the traditional order were altered. So everything remained as it was.[4]

In Japan as in France, worn-out parents, exhausted young people,
employers disappointed by the products of an education which
they find ill suited to their needs, are all the helpless victims of
a mechanism which is nothing but the cumulative effect of their
own strategies, engendered and amplified by the logic of competition of everyone against everyone.

This might have been the place to reply to the mangling and mis-
representation of my works by certain misguided or ill-disposed
analysts, but I would have needed time to show how the logic of
the scholastic component of the mode of reproduction – notably,
its *statistical* character – and its characteristic *contradictions* may
be, and *without contradiction*, at the root of the reproduction of
the structures of advanced societies and of a good many of the
changes that affect them. These contradictions (which I analyzed
in the chapter of *Distinction* titled "Classes and Classifications")
no doubt constitute the hidden principle of certain political conflicts characteristic of the recent period, such as the events of
May 1968, which rocked the French and Japanese universities at
almost the same time, the same causes producing the same effects,
without our being able to point to any direct influence. I have
undertaken a lengthy analysis, in another study which I entitled
somewhat derisively *Homo Academicus*,[5] of the factors that determined the crisis of the scholastic world, the visible expression of
which were the events of May 1968: overproduction and devaluation of diplomas (two phenomena which, if I am to believe what
I read, also concern Japan); devaluation of university positions,
especially subordinate positions, which have grown in numbers
without a proportional opening up of careers because of the quite
archaic structure of the university hierarchy (here again, I would
like to make a comparative inquiry into the forms that the relations

of university time and power, as I have analyzed them in France, assume in the case of Japan).

And I think that it is in the changes of the scholastic field and, especially, of the relations between the scholastic field and the economic field, in the transformation of the correspondence between academic qualifications and posts, that we might find the real principle behind the new social movements which have appeared in France, in the aftermath of '68 and also more recently, such as the very new phenomenon of *coordinations*,[6] which, if I may believe my sources, are also beginning to emerge in Germany and Japan, notably among young workers, who are less devoted than their elders to the traditional work ethic. Likewise, the political changes which can now be observed in the USSR, and which are beginning in China, are no doubt linked to the considerable increase in the numbers of high school graduates in these countries, giving rise to contradictions, first of all, in the very midst of the field of power itself.

But it would also be necessary to study the link between the new school delinquency, which is more widespread in Japan than in France, and the logic of furious competition which dominates the school institution, especially the *effect of a final verdict or destiny* that the educational system exerts over teenagers. Often with a psychological brutality which nothing can attenuate, the school institution lays down its final judgments and its verdicts, from which there is no appeal, ranking all students in a unique hierarchy of forms of excellence, nowadays dominated by a single discipline, mathematics. Those who are excluded are condemned in the name of a collectively recognized and accepted criterion (and thus one which is psychologically unquestionable and unquestioned), the criterion of intelligence. Therefore, in order to restore an identity in jeopardy, students have no recourse except to make a violent break with the scholastic order and the social order (it has been observed, in France, that it is their collective opposition to school that tends to weld delinquents into gangs) or, as is also the case, to suffer psychological crisis, even mental illness or suicide.

Finally, one should analyze all the technical dysfunctions which, from the point of view of the system itself, that is, strictly from the point of view of technical efficiency (in the school institution and beyond), result from the primacy accorded to *social reproduction* strategies. I shall just cite, by way of example, the low status which families objectively assign to technical education and the privilege they confer on general education. It is probable that, in Japan as in France, those leaders who, coming themselves from the great public universities in Japan or from the Grandes Écoles in France, advocate the revaluation of a technical education which has been reduced to the state of "fall-back" or dumping-ground (and which, especially in Japan, also suffers from the competition of business schools) would regard as catastrophic the relegation of their own sons to technical schools. And the same contradiction is to be found in the ambivalence of these same leaders toward an educational system to which they owe, if not their positions, at least the authority and the legitimacy with which they occupy those positions. As if they wanted to have the technical benefits of the scholastic operation without assuming any of the social costs, such as the exigencies associated with the possession of what might be regarded as universal titles, as distinct from those "house" titles that businesses award, they promote private education and support or inspire political initiatives aimed at reducing the autonomy of the school institution and the liberty of the teaching profession. They manifest the greatest ambiguity in the debate on specialization in education, as if they wanted to enjoy the benefits of all the options at once: the limits and guarantees associated with a highly specialized education, but also the broad-mindedness and detachment facilitated by a general cultural education, favoring the development of an adaptability appropriate to mobile and "flexible" employees; the certainty and self-confidence of the young executives produced by the École Nationale d'Administration or Todaï, those levelheaded managers of stable situations, but also the daring of the young hustlers who, having risen above their rank, are supposed to be better adapted to times of crisis.

But, if the sociologist may be allowed this once to make a prediction, it is undoubtedly in the increasingly tense relationship between the great and minor state nobility that one should expect to find the underlying principle of future major conflicts. Everything points to the supposition that, facing an ever more tenacious monopoly of all the highest positions of power – in banking, industry, politics – on the part of the old boys of the Grandes Écoles in France, of the great public universities in Japan, the holders of second-class titles, the lesser samurai of culture, will be led, in their struggle for an enlargement of the circles of power, to invoke new universalist justifications, much as the minor provincial nobles did in France from the sixteenth century to the beginnings of the French Revolution, or as did the excluded lesser samurai who, in the name of "liberty and civil rights," led the revolt against the nineteenth-century Meiji reform.

Notes

This is the text of a lecture delivered at the University of Todaï in October 1989. It was originally subtitled "Introduction to a Japanese reading of *The State Nobility*."

1 Two private schools especially dedicated to intensive preparation for the major competitive examinations. *Trans.*
2 Pierre Bourdieu, *The State Nobility: Elite Schools in the Field of Power*, trans. Lauretta C. Clough (Cambridge: Polity Press, 1996).
3 Advanced business school. *Trans.*
4 Norbert Elias, *The Court Society* (1975), trans. Edmund Jephcott (Oxford: Blackwell, 1983), p. 87.
5 Pierre Bourdieu, *Homo Academicus*, trans. Peter Collier (Cambridge: Polity Press, 1990).
6 "Coordinations" refers to a new form of organization and mobilization which appeared in the mid-1980s on the occasion of the nurses' demonstrations and subsequently the demonstrations of school pupils and higher education students, and which aimed to establish a relation between leaders and activists different from those in traditional trade unions. *Trans.*

APPENDIX

Social Space and Field of Power

Why does it seem necessary and legitimate for me to introduce the notions of social space and field of power into the lexicon of sociology? In the first place, to break with the tendency to think of the social world in a substantialist manner. The notion of *space* contains, in itself, the principle of a *relational* understanding of the social world. It affirms that every "reality" it designates resides in the *mutual exteriority* of its composite elements. Apparent, directly visible beings, whether individuals or groups, exist and subsist in and through *difference*; that is, they occupy *relative positions* in a space of relations which, although invisible and always difficult to show empirically, is the most real reality (the *ens realissimum*, as scholasticism would say) and the real principle of the behavior of individuals and groups.

The primary objective of social science is not to construct classes. The problem of classification, which is common to all sciences, is only posed in such a dramatic way to the social sciences because it is a political problem, which in practice arises in the logic of political struggle every time one seeks to construct real groups through mobilization, the paradigm of which is the Marxist ambition to construct the proletariat as a historical force ("Workers of the world, *unite*"). A scientist and man of action, Marx provided false theoretical solutions – such as the affirmation of the real existence of classes – for a true practical problem: the need for every political action to demand the capability, real or supposed, in any case *credible*, to express the interests of a group; to demonstrate – this is one of the primary functions of demonstrations – the existence of that group and the actual or potential social force it is capable of bringing to those who experience it and thus constitute it as a group. To speak of social space is thus to solve, by making it disappear, the problem of the existence or nonexistence of classes which has divided sociologists from the outset. One cannot deny the existence of classes without also denying the essential element of that which the notion's defenders seek to affirm by using it, namely *social differentiation*, which may generate individual antagonisms and, at times, collective confrontations between agents situated in different positions in social space.

Social science should construct not classes, but rather the social spaces in which classes can be demarcated, but which only exist on paper. In each case it should *construct and discover* (beyond the opposition between constructionism and realism) the principle of differentiation which permits one to reengender theoretically the empirically observed social space. Nothing permits one to assume that the principle of difference is the same at all times and in all places, in Ming China and contemporary China, or in today's Germany, Russia and Algeria. But with the exception of the least differentiated societies (which still present differences in symbolic capital, which are more difficult to measure), all societies appear as social spaces, that is, as structures of differences that can only be understood by constructing the generative principle which objectively grounds those differences. This principle is none other than the structure of the distribution of the forms of power or the kinds of capital which are effective in the social universe under consideration – and which vary according to the specific place and moment at hand.

This structure is not immutable, and the topology that describes a state of the social positions permits a dynamic analysis of the conservation and transformation of the structure of the active properties' distribution and thus of the social space itself. That is what I mean when I describe the global social space as a *field*, that is, both as a field of forces, whose necessity is imposed on agents who are engaged in it, and as a field of struggles within which agents confront each other, with differentiated means and ends according to their position in the structure of the field of forces, thus contributing to conserving or transforming its structure.

Something like a class or, more generally, a group mobilized by and through the defense of its interests, can only come to exist at the cost and at the end of a collective work of construction which is inseparably theoretical and practical. But not all social groupings are equally probable, and this social artifact which is always a social group has all the more chances of existing and durably subsisting if the assembled agents who construct it are already close to each other in the social space (this is also true of a unity based on an affective relationship of love or friendship, whether or not it is socially sanctioned). In other words, the symbolic work of *constitution* or consecration that is necessary to create a unified group (imposition of names, acronyms, of rallying signs, public demonstrations, etc.) is all the more likely to succeed if the social agents on which it is exerted are more inclined, because of their proximity in the space of social positions and also because of the dispositions and interests associated with those positions, to mutually recognize each other and recognize themselves in the same project (political or otherwise).

But by accepting the idea of a unified social space, aren't we committing a *petitio principii*? Wouldn't it be necessary to ask about the social conditions of possibility and the limits of such a space? In fact, the genesis of the state is inseparable from the process of unification of the different social, economic, cultural (or educational), and political fields which goes hand in hand with the progressive constitution of the state monopoly of legitimate physical and *symbolic* violence. Because it concentrates an ensemble of material and symbolic resources, the state is in a position to regulate the functioning of the different fields, whether through financial intervention (such as public support of investment in the economic field, or, in the cultural field, support for one kind of education or another) or through juridical intervention (such as the different regulations concerning organizations or the behavior of individual agents).

I introduced the notion of the field of power to account for structural effects which are not otherwise easily understood, especially certain properties of the practices and representations of writers or artists, which references to the literary or artistic field alone could not completely explain. For example, the double ambiguity in relation to the "people" and the "bourgeois," which is found in writers or artists occupying different positions in the field, only becomes intelligible if one considers the dominated position that fields of cultural production occupy in the larger social space.

The field of power (which should not be confused with the polit-ical field) is not a field like the others. It is the space of the relations of force between the different kinds of capital or, more precisely, between the agents who possess a sufficient amount of one of the different kinds of capital to be in a position to dominate the cor-responding field, whose struggles intensify whenever the relative value of the different kinds of capital is questioned (for example, the exchange rate between cultural capital and economic capital); that is, especially when the established equilibrium in the field of instances specifically charged with the reproduction of the field of power is threatened (in the French case, the field of the Grandes Écoles).

One of the stakes of the struggles which oppose the set of agents or institutions which have in common the possession of a suffi-cient quantity of specific capital (especially economic or cultural) to occupy dominant positions within their respective fields is the conservation or transformation of the "exchange rate" between different kinds of capital and, along the same lines, control of the bureaucratic instances which are in a position to modify the ex-change rate through administrative measures (those, for example, which can affect the rarity of academic titles opening access to dominant positions and, thus, the relative values of those titles and the corresponding positions). The forces which can be engaged in those struggles and the orientation – conservative or subversive – which is applied to them, depend on the "exchange rate" between the different kinds of capital, that is, on the very thing the struggles seek to conserve or transform.

Domination is not the direct and simple action exercised by a set of agents ("the dominant class") invested with powers of coer-cion. Rather, it is the indirect effect of a complex set of actions engendered within the network of intersecting constraints which each of the dominants, thus dominated by the structure of the field through which domination is exerted, endures on behalf of all the others.

3

Rethinking the State:
Genesis and Structure of
the Bureaucratic Field

To endeavor to think the state is to take the risk of taking over (or being taken over by) a thought of the state, that is, of applying to the state categories of thought produced and guaranteed by the state and hence to misrecognize its most profound truth. This proposition, which may seem both abstract and preemptory, will be more readily accepted if, at the close of the argument, one agrees to return to this point of departure, but armed this time with the knowledge that one of the major powers of the state is to produce and impose (especially through the school system) categories of thought that we spontaneously apply to all things of the social world – including the state itself.

However, to give a first and more intuitive grasp of this analysis and to expose the danger of always being thought by a state that we believe we are thinking, I would like to cite a passage from *Alte Meister Komödie* by Thomas Bernhard:

School is the state school where young people are turned into state persons and thus into nothing other than henchmen of the state. Walking to school, I was walking into the state and, since the state destroys people, into the institution for the destruction of people . . . The state forced me, like everyone else, into myself, and made me compliant towards it, the state, and turned me into a state person, regulated and registered and trained and finished and perverted and dejected, like everyone else. When we see people, we only see state people, the state servants, as we quite rightly say, who serve the state all their lives and thus serve unnature all their lives.[1]

The idiosyncratic rhetoric of Thomas Bernhard, one of excess and of hyperbole in anathema, is well suited to my intention, which is to subject the state and the thought of the state to a sort of *hyperbolic doubt*. For, when it comes to the state, one never doubts enough. And, though literary exaggeration always risks self-effacement by de-realizing itself in its very excess, one should take what Thomas Bernhard says seriously: to have any chance of thinking a state that still thinks itself through those who attempt to think it (as in the case of Hegel or Durkheim), one must strive to question all the presuppositions and preconstructions inscribed in the reality under analysis as well as in the very thoughts of the analyst.

The difficult and perhaps interminable work that is necessary to break with preconceptions and presuppositions – that is, with all theses that are never stated as such because they are inscribed in the obviousness of ordinary experience, with the entire sub-stratum of the unthinkable that underlies the most vigilant thinking – is often misunderstood, and not only by those whose conservat-ism it shocks. In fact, there is a tendency to reduce what is and should be an *epistemological* questioning to a *political* questioning inspired by prejudices or political impulses (anarchist dispositions in the specific case of the state, iconoclastic passions of relativist philistines in art, antidemocratic inclinations in public opinion). It is quite probable, as Didier Eribon has effectively shown in the case of Michel Foucault, that this *epistemic radicalism* is rooted in subversive impulses and dispositions, which it sublimates and transcends. Insofar as one is led to question not only "moral conformism," but also "logical conformism," that is, the basic structures of thought, one goes against both those who, finding no fault with the world as it is, see in this epistemic radicalism a kind of decisive and socially irresponsible preconceived opinion, as well as those who reduce it to political radicalism as they conceive it, that is, to a denunciation which, in more than one case, is a particularly perverse way of sheltering oneself from true epistemological questioning. (I could give an infinite number of examples to show how "radical" critiques of the categories of INSEE[2] in the name of a Marxist theory of classes have allowed critics to avoid an epistemological critique of those same categories and of the act of categorization or classification, or even how denouncing the complicity of the "philosophy of state" with the bureaucratic order or with the "bourgeoisie" gives free rein to the effects of all the epistemic distortions inscribed in the "scholastic point of view.") The real symbolic revolutions are without doubt those which, more than moral conformism, violate logical conformism, unleashing merciless repression which gives rise to similar attacks against mental integrity.

To show both the difficulty and the necessity of a rupture with state-thought, present in the most intimate of our thoughts, one could analyze the battle recently declared – in the midst of the Gulf War – in France about a seemingly insignificant topic: orthography. Correct spelling, designated and guaranteed as normal by law, that is, by the state, is a social artifact only imperfectly founded upon logical or even linguistic reason; it is the product of a work of normalization and codification, quite analogous to that which the state effects concurrently in other realms of social life.[3] Now, when, at a particular moment, the state or any of its representatives undertakes a reform of orthography (as was done, with similar effects, a century ago), that is, to undo by decree what the state had ordered by decree, this immediately triggers the indignant protest of a good number of those whose status depends on "writing," in its most common sense but also in the sense given to it by writers. And remarkably, all those defenders of orthographic orthodoxy mobilize in the name of *natural* spelling and of the satisfaction, experienced as intrinsically aesthetic, given by the perfect agreement between mental structures and objective structures – between the mental forms socially instituted in minds through the teaching of correct spelling and the reality designated by words rightfully spelled. For those who possess spelling to the point where they are possessed by it, the perfectly arbitrary "ph" of the word "nénuphar" has become so evidently inextricable from the flower it designates that they can, in all good faith, invoke nature and the *natural* to denounce an intervention of the state aimed at reducing the arbitrariness of a spelling which itself is, in all evidence, the product of an earlier arbitrary intervention of the same.

One could offer countless similar instances in which the effects of choices made by the state have so completely impressed themselves in reality and in minds that possibilities initially discarded have become totally unthinkable (for instance, a system of domestic production of electricity analogous to that of home heating). Thus, if the mildest attempt to modify school programs, and especially timetables for the different disciplines, almost always and everywhere encounters great resistance, it is not only because powerful occupational interests (such as those of the teaching staff) are attached to the established academic order. It is also because matters of culture, and in particular the social divisions and hierarchies associated with them, are constituted as such by the actions of the state which, by instituting them both in things and in minds, confers upon the cultural arbitrary all the appearances of the natural.

A Radical Doubt

It is in the realm of symbolic production that the grip of the state is felt most powerfully. State bureaucracies and their representatives are great producers of "social problems" that social science does little more than ratify whenever it takes them over as "sociological" problems. (To demonstrate this, it would suffice to plot the amount of research, varying across countries and periods, devoted to problems of the state, such as poverty, immigration, educational failure, more or less rephrased in scientific language.)

Yet the best proof of the fact that the thought of the bureaucratic thinker (*penseur fonctionnaire*) is pervaded by the official representation of the official is no doubt the power of seduction wielded by those representations of the state (as in Hegel) that portray bureaucracy as a "universal group" endowed with the intuition of, and a will to, universal interest; or as an "organ of reflection" and a rational instrument in charge of realizing the general interest (as with Durkheim, in spite of his great prudence on the matter).[4]

The specific difficulty that shrouds this question lies in the fact that, behind the appearance of thinking it, most of the writings devoted to the state partake, more or less efficaciously and directly, of the *construction* of the state, that is, of its very existence. This is particularly true of all juridical writings which, especially during the phase of construction and consolidation, take their full meaning not only as theoretical contributions to the knowledge of the state but also as political strategies aimed at imposing a particular vision of the state, a vision in agreement with the interests and values associated with the particular position of those who produce them in the emerging bureaucratic universe (this is often forgotten by the best historical works, such as those of the Cambridge school).

From its inception, social science itself has been part and parcel of this work of construction of the representation of the state which makes up part of the reality of the state itself. All the issues raised about bureaucracy, such as those of neutrality and disinterestedness, are posed also about sociology itself – only at a higher degree of difficulty since there arises in addition the question of the latter's autonomy from the state.

It is therefore the task of the history of the social sciences to uncover all the unconscious ties to the social world that the social sciences owe to the history which has produced them (and which are recorded in their problematics, theories, methods, concepts, etc.). Thus one discovers, in particular, that social science in the modern sense of the term is intimately linked to social struggles and socialism, but less as a direct expression of these movements and of their theoretical ramifications than as an answer to the problems that these struggles formulated and brought forth. Social science finds its first advocates among the philanthropists and the reformers, that is, in the enlightened avant-garde of the dominant who expect that "social economics" (as an auxiliary science to political science) will provide them with a solution to "social problems" and particularly to those posed by individuals and groups "with problems."

A comparative survey of the development of the social sciences suggests that a model designed to explain the historical and cross-national variations of these disciplines should take into account two fundamental factors. The first is the fact that the form assumed by the social demand for knowledge of the social world depends, among other things, on the philosophy dominant within state bureaucracies (such as the liberalism of Keynesianism). Thus a powerful state demand may ensure conditions propitious to the development of a social science relatively independent from economic forces (and of the direct claims of the dominant) – but strongly dependent upon the state. The second factor is the degree of autonomy both of the educational system and of the scientific

field from the dominant political and economic forces, an autonomy that undoubtedly requires both a strong outgrowth of social
movements and of the social critique of established powers as well
as a high degree of independence of social scientists from these
movements.

History attests that the social sciences can increase their independence from the pressures of social demand – which is a major
precondition of their progress toward scientificity – only by increasing their reliance upon the state. And thus they run the risk
of losing their autonomy from the state, unless they are prepared
to use against the state the (relative) freedom that it grants them.

The Concentration of Capital

To sum up the results of the analysis by way of anticipation, I
would say, using a variation around Max Weber's famous formula, that the state is an X (to be determined) which successfully
claims the monopoly of the legitimate use of physical and *symbolic* violence over a definite territory and over the totality of the
corresponding population. If the state is able to exert symbolic
violence, it is because it incarnates itself simultaneously in objectivity, in the form of specific organizational structures and mechanisms, and in subjectivity, in the form of mental structures and
categories of perception and thought. By realizing itself in social
structures and in the mental structures adapted to them, the instituted institution makes us forget that it issues out of a long series
of acts of *institution* (in the active sense) and hence has all the
appearances of the *natural*.

This is why there is no more potent tool for rupture than the
reconstruction of genesis: by bringing back into view the conflicts
and confrontations of the early beginnings and therefore all the
discarded possibles, it retrieves the possibility that things could
have been (and still could be) otherwise. And, through such a practical utopia, it questions the "possible" which, among all others,
was actualized. Breaking with the temptation of the analysis of
essence, but without renouncing for that the intention of uncovering invariants, I would like to outline *a model of the emergence
of the state* designed to offer a systematic account of the properly
historical logic of the processes which have led to the institution

of this "X" we call the state. Such a project is most difficult, impossible indeed, for it demands joining the rigor and coherence of theoretical construction with submission to the almost boundless data accumulated by historical research. To suggest the complexity of such a task, I will simply cite one historian, who, because he stays within the limits of his specialty, evokes it only partially himself:

> The most neglected zones of history have been border zones, as for instance the borders between specialties. Thus, the study of government requires knowledge of the theory of government (i.e., of the history of political thought), knowledge of the practice of government (i.e., of the history of institutions) and finally knowledge of governmental personnel (i.e., of social history). Now, few historians are capable of moving across these specialties with equal ease . . . There are other border zones of history that would also require study, such as warfare technology at the beginning of the modern period. Without a better knowledge of such problems, it is difficult to measure the importance of the logistical effort undertaken by such government in a given campaign. However, these technical problems should not be investigated solely from the standpoint of the military historian as traditionally defined. The military historian must also be a historian of government. In the history of public finances and taxation, too, many unknowns remain. Here again the specialist must be more than a narrow historian of finances, in the old meaning of the word; he must be a historian of government and an economist. Unfortunately, such a task has not been helped by the fragmentation of history into subfields, each with its monopoly of specialists, and by the feeling that certain aspects of history are fashionable while others are not.[5]

The state is the *culmination of a process of concentration of different species of capital*: capital of physical force or instruments of coercion (army, police), economic capital, cultural or (better) informational capital, and symbolic capital. It is this concentration as such which constitutes the state as the holder of a sort of metacapital granting power over other species of capital and over their holders. Concentration of the different species of capital (which proceeds hand in hand with the construction of the corresponding fields) leads indeed to the *emergence* of a specific, properly statist capital (*capital étatique*) which enables the state to exercise power over the different fields and over the different particular species of capital, and especially over the rates of conversion between them (and thereby over the relations of force between their respective holders). It follows that the construction of the state proceeds apace with the construction of a *field of power*, defined as the space of play within which the holders of capital (of different species) struggle *in particular* for power over the state, that is, over the statist capital granting power over the different species of capital and over their reproduction (particularly through the school system).

Although the different dimensions of this process of concentration (armed forces, taxation, law, etc.) are *interdependent*, for purposes of exposition and analysis I will examine each in turn.

From the Marxist models which tend to treat the state as a mere organ of coercion to Max Weber's classical definition, or from Norbert Elias's to Charles Tilly's formulations, most models of the genesis of the state have privileged the concentration of the capital of physical force.[6] To say that the forces of coercion (army and police) are becoming concentrated is to say that the institutions mandated to guarantee order are progressively being separated from the ordinary social world; that physical violence can only be applied by a specialized group, centralized and disciplined, especially mandated for such an end and clearly identified as such within society; that the professional army progressively causes the disappearance of feudal troops, thereby directly threatening the nobility in its statutory monopoly of the warring function. (One should acknowledge here the merit of Norbert Elias – too often erroneously credited, particularly among historians, for ideas and theories that belong to the broader heritage of sociology – for having drawn out all the implications of Weber's analysis by showing that the state could not have succeeded in progressively establishing its monopoly over violence without dispossessing its domestic competitors of instruments of physical violence and of the right to use them, thereby contributing to the emergence of one of the most essential dimensions of the "civilizing process.")[7]

The emerging state must assert its physical force in two different contexts: first externally, in relation to *other actual or potential states* (foreign princes), in and through war for land (which led to the creation of powerful armies); and second internally, in relation to rival powers (princes and lords) and to resistance from below (dominated classes). The armed forces progressively differentiate themselves with, on the one hand, military forces destined for interstate competition and, on the other hand, police forces destined for the maintenance of intrastate order.[8]

Concentration of the capital of physical force requires the establishment of an efficient fiscal system, which in turn proceeds in tandem with the unification of economic space (creation of a national market). The levies raised by the dynastic state apply equally to all subjects – and not, as with feudal levies, only to dependants who may in turn tax their own men. Appearing in the last decade of the twelfth century, state tax developed in tandem with the growth of *war expenses*. The imperatives of territorial defense, first invoked instance by instance, slowly become the permanent justification of the "obligatory" and "regular" character of the levies perceived "without limitation of time other than that regularly assigned by the king" and directly or indirectly applicable "to all social groups."

Thus was progressively established a specific economic logic, founded on *levies without counterpart* and *redistribution* functioning as the basis for the conversion of economic capital into symbolic capital, concentrated at first in the person of the Prince.[9] The institution of the tax (over and against the resistance of the taxpayers) stands in a relation of *circular causality* with the development of the armed forces necessary for the expansion and defense of the territory under coutrol, and thus for the levying of tributes and taxes as well as for imposing via constraint the payment of that tax. The institution of the tax was the result of a veritable *internal war* waged by the agents of the state against the resistance of the subjects, who discover themselves as such mainly if not exclusively by discovering themselves as taxable, as tax payers (*contribuables*). Royal ordinances imposed four degrees of repression in cases of a delay in collection: seizures; arrests for debt (*les contraintes par corps*), including imprisonment; a writ of restraint binding on all parties (*contraintes solidaires*); and the quartering of soldiers. It follows that the *question of the legitimacy* of the tax cannot but be raised (Norbert Elias correctly remarks that, at its inception, taxation presents itself as a kind of racket). It is only progressively that we come to conceive taxes as a necessary tribute to the needs of a recipient that transcends the king, that is, this "fictive body" that is the state.

Even today, *tax fraud* bears testimony to the fact that the legitimacy of taxation is not wholly taken for granted. It is well known that in the initial phase armed resistance against it was not considered disobedience to royal ordinances but a morally legitimate defense of the rights of the family against a tax system wherein one could not recognize the just and paternal monarch.[10] From the lease (*ferme*) concluded in due and good form with the Royal Treasury, to the last underlessee (*sous-fermier*) in charge of local levies, a whole hierarchy of leases and subleases was interposed as reminders of the suspicion of alienation of tax and of usurpation of authority, constantly reactivated by a whole chain of small collectors, often badly paid and suspected of corruption both by their victims and by higher ranking officials.[11] The recognition of an entity transcending the agents in charge of its implementation – whether royalty or the state – thus insulated from profane critique, no doubt found a practical basis in the dissociation of the king from the unjust and corrupt agents who cheated him as much as they cheated the people.[12]

The concentration of armed forces and of the financial resources necessary to maintain them does not happen without the concentration of a symbolic capital of recognition (or legitimacy). It matters that the body of agents responsible for collecting taxation without profiting from it and the methods of government and management they use (accounting, filing, verdicts on disagreements, procedural acts, oversight of operations, etc.) be in a position to be known and recognized as such, that they be "easily identified with the person, with the dignity of power." Thus "bailiffs wear its *livery*, enjoy the authority of its *emblems* and signify their commands in its name." It matters also that the average taxpayer be in a position "to recognize the liveries of the guards, the signs of the sentry boxes" and to distinguish the "keepers of leases," those agents of hated and despised financiers, from the royal guards of the mounted constabulary, from the Prévôté de l'Hôtel or the Gardes du Corps regarded as inviolable because their jackets bear the royal colors.[13]

All authors agree that the progessive development of the recognition of the legitimacy of official taxation is bound up with the rise of a form of nationalism. And, indeed, the broad-based collection of taxes has likely contributed to the unification of the territory or, to be more precise, to the construction, both in reality and in representation, of the state as a *unitary territory*, as a reality unified by its submission to the same obligations, themselves imposed by the imperatives of defense. It is also probable that this "national" consciousness developed first among the members of the *representative institutions* that emerged alongside the debate over taxation. Indeed, we know that these authorities were more inclined to consent to taxation whenever the latter seemed to them to spring, not from the private interests of the prince, but from the *interests of the country* (and, first among them, from the requirement of territorial *defense*). The state progressively inscribes itself in a space that is not yet the national space it will later become but that already presents itself as a *fount of sovereignty*, with for example the monopoly of the right to coin money, and as the basis of a transcendent symbolic value.[14]

The concentration of economic capital linked to the establishment of unified taxation is paralleled by a concentration of *informational capital* (of which cultural capital is one dimension) which is itself correlated with the unification of the cultural market. Thus, very early on, public authorities carried out surveys of the state of resources (for example, as early as 1194, there were "appraisals of quarter master sergeants" and a census of the carriages (*charrois*) and armed men that 83 cities and royal abbeys had to provide when the king convened his *ost*; in 1221, an embryo of a budget and a registry of receipts and expenditures appear). The state concentrates, treats, and redistributes information and, most of all, effects a *theoretical unification*. Taking the vantage point of the Whole, of society in its totality, the state claims responsibility for all operations of *totalization* (especially thanks to census-taking and statistics or national accounting) and of *objectivization*, through cartography (the unitary representation of space from above) or more simply through writing as an instrument of accumulation of knowledge (archives, for example), as well as for all operations of *codification* as cognitive unification implying centralization and monopolization in the hands of clerks and men of letters.

Culture[15] is unifying: the state contributes to the unification of the cultural market by unifying all codes, linguistic and juridical, and by effecting a homogenization of all forms of communication, including bureaucratic communication (through forms, official notices, etc.). Through classification systems (especially according to sex and age) inscribed in law, through bureaucratic procedures, educational structures and social rituals (particularly salient in the case of Japan and England), the state molds *mental structures* and imposes common principles of vision and division, forms of thinking that are to the civilized mind what the primitive forms of classification described by Mauss and Durkheim were to the "savage mind." And it thereby contributes to the construction of what is commonly designated as national identity (or, in a more traditional language, national character).[16]

By universally imposing and inculcating (within the limits of its authority) a dominant culture thus constituted as *legitimate national* culture, the school system, through the teaching of history (and especially the history of literature), inculcates the foundations of a true "civic religion" and more precisely, the fundamental presuppositions of the national self-image. Derek Sayer and Philip Corrigan show how the English partake very widely – well beyond the boundaries of the dominant class – of the cult of a doubly particular culture, at once bourgeois and national, with for instance the myth of *Englishness*, understood as a set of undefinable and inimitable qualities (for the non-English), "reasonableness," "moderation," "pragmatism," hostility to ideology, "quirkiness," and "eccentricity."[17] This is very visible in the case of England, which has perpetuated with extraordinary continuity a very ancient tradition (as with juridical rituals or the cult of the royal family for example), or in the case of Japan, where the invention of a national culture is directly tied to the invention of the state. In the case of France, the nationalist dimension of culture is masked under a universalist facade. The propensity to conceive the annexation to one's national culture as a means of acceding to universality is at the basis of both the brutally integrative vision of the republican tradition (nourished by the founding myth of the universal revolution) and very perverse forms of universalist imperialism and of internationalist nationalism.[18]

Cultural and linguistic unification is accompanied by the imposition of the dominant language and culture as legitimate and by the rejection of all other languages into indignity (thus demoted as patois or local dialects). By rising to universality, a particular culture or language causes all others to fall into particularity. What is more, given that the universalization of requirements thus officially instituted does not come with a universalization of access to the means needed to fulfill them, this fosters both the monopolization of the universal by the few and the dispossession of all others, who are, in a way, thereby mutilated in their humanity.

Symbolic Capital

Everything points to the concentration of a symbolic capital of recognized authority which, though it has been ignored by all the existing theories of the genesis of the state, appears as the condition or, at minimum, the correlate of all the other forms of concentration, insofar as they endure at all. Symbolic capital is any property (any form of capital whether physical, economic, cultural or social) when it is perceived by social agents endowed with categories of perception which cause them to know it and to recognize it, to give it value. (For example, the concept of honor in Mediterranean societies is a typical form of symbolic capital which exists only through repute, that is, through the representation that others have of it to the extent that they share a set of beliefs liable to cause them to perceive and appreciate certain patterns of conduct as honorable or dishonorable.)[19] More precisely, symbolic capital is the form taken by any species of capital whenever it is perceived through categories of perception that are the product of the embodiment of divisions or of oppositions inscribed in the structure of the distribution of this species of capital (strong/weak, large/small, rich/poor, cultured/uncultured). It follows that the state, which possesses the means of imposition and inculcation of the durable principles of vision and division that conform to its own structure, is the site par excellence of the concentration and exercise of symbolic power.

The process of concentration of juridical capital, an objectified and codified form of symbolic capital, follows its *own logic* distinct from that of the concentration of military capital and of financial capital. In the twelfth and thirteenth centuries, several legal systems coexisted in Europe, with, on the one hand, ecclesiastical jurisdictions, as represented by Christian courts, and, on the other, secular jurisdictions, including the justice of the king, the justice of the lords, and the jurisdiction of *municipalités* (cities), of corporations, and of trade.[20] The jurisdiction of the lord as justice was exercised only over his vassals and all those who resided on his lands (that is, noble vassals, with non-noble free persons and serfs falling under a different set of rules). In the beginning, the king had jurisdiction only over the royal domain and legislated only in trials concerning his direct vassals and the inhabitants of his own fiefdoms. But, as Marc Bloch remarked, royal justice soon slowly "infiltrated" the whole of society.[21] Though it was not the product of an intention, and even less so of a purposeful plan, no more than it was the object of collusion among those who benefited from it (including the king and the jurists), the movement of concentration always followed one and the same trajectory, eventually leading to the creation of a juridical apparatus. This movement started with the provost marshals mentioned in the "testament of Philippe Auguste" in 1190 and with the bailiffs, these higher officers of royalty who held solemn assizes and controlled the provosts. It continued under St Louis with the creation of different bureaucratic entities, the Conseil d'État (Council of State), the Cours des Comptes (Court of Accounts), and the judiciary court (Curia Regis) which took the name of Parlement. Thanks to the appeal procedure, the Parlement, a sedentary body composed exclusively of lawyers, became one of the major instruments for the concentration of juridical power in the hands of the king.

Royal justice slowly corralled the majority of criminal cases which had previously belonged to the tribunals of lords or of churches. "Royal cases," those in which the rights of royalty are infringed (as with crimes of lese-majesty: counterfeiting of money, forgery of the seal), came increasingly to be reserved for royal bailiffs. More especially, jurists elaborated a *theory of appeal* which submitted all the jurisdictions of the kingdom to the king. Whereas feudal courts were sovereign, it now became admitted that any judgment delivered by a lord upholder of law could be deferred before the king by the injured party if deemed contrary to the customs of the country. This procedure, called *supplication*, slowly turned into appeal. Self-appointed judges progressively disappeared from feudal courts to be replaced by professional jurists, the officers of justice. The appeal followed the ladder of authority: appeal was made from the inferior lord to the lord of higher rank and from the duke or the count to the king (it was not possible to skip a level and, for instance, appeal directly to the king).

By relying on the *specific interest of the jurists* (a typical example of interest in the universal) who, as we shall see, elaborated all sorts of legitimating theories according to which the king represents the common interest and owes everybody security and justice, the royalty limited the competence of feudal jurisdictions (it proceeded similarly with ecclesiastical jurisdictions, for instance by limiting the church's right of asylum). The process of *concentration* of juridical capital was paralleled by a process of *differentiation* which led to the constitution of an autonomous juridical field.[22] The *judiciary body* grew organized and hierarchized: provosts became the ordinary judges of ordinary cases; bailiffs and seneschals became sedentary; they were assisted more and more by lieutenants who became irrevocable officers of justice and who gradually superseded the bailiffs, thus relegated to purely honorific functions. In the fourteenth century, we witness the appearance of a *public ministry* in charge of official suits. The king now has state prosecutors who act in his name and slowly become functionaries.

The ordinance of 1670 completed the process of concentration which progressively stripped the lordly and ecclesiastical jurisdictions of their powers in favor of royal jurisdictions. It ratified the progressive conquests of jurists: the competence of the place of the crime became the rule; the precedence of royal judges over those of lords was affirmed. The ordinance also enumerated royal cases and annulled ecclesiastical and communal privileges by stipulating that judges of appeal should always be royal judges. In brief, the competence delegated over a certain *ressort* (territory) replaced statutory precedence or authority exercised directly over persons.

Later on the construction of the juridico-bureaucratic structures constitutive of the state proceeded alongside the construction of the body of jurists and of what Sarah Hanley calls the "Family-State Compact," this covenant struck between the state and the corporation of jurists which constituted itself as such by exerting strict control over its own reproduction. "The Family-State Compact provided a formidable family model of socio-economic authority which influenced the state model of political power in the making at the same time."[23]

The concentration of juridical capital is one aspect, quite fundamental, of a larger process of concentration of symbolic capital in its different forms. This capital is the basis of the specific authority of the holder of state power and in particular of a very mysterious power, namely his power of nomination. Thus, for example, the king attempts to control the totality of the traffic in *honors* to which "gentlemen" may lay claim. He strives to extend his mastery over the great ecclesiastical prerogatives, the orders of chivalry, the distribution of military and court offices and, last but not least, titles of nobility. Thus is a *central authority of nomination* gradually constituted.

One remembers the nobles of Aragon, mentioned by V. G. Kiernan, who called themselves *ricoshombres de natura*: gentlemen by nature or by birth, in contrast to the nobles created by the king. This distinction, which clearly played a role in the struggles within the nobility or between nobility and royal power, is of utmost importance. It opposes two modes of access to nobility: the first, called "natural," is nothing other than heredity and public recognition (by other nobles as well as by "commoners"); the second, "legal nobility," is the result of ennoblement by the king. The two forms of consecration coexist for a long time. Arlette Jouanna clearly shows that, with the concentration of the power of ennoblement in the hands of the king, *statutory honor*, founded on the recognition of peers and of others and affirmed and defended by challenge and prowess, slowly gives way to *honors attributed by the state*.[24] Such honors, like any fiduciary currencies, have currency and value on all the markets controlled by the state. As the king concentrates greater and greater quantities of symbolic capital (Mousnier called them *fidélités, "loyalties"*),[25] his power to distribute symbolic capital in the form of offices and honors conceived as rewards increases continually. The symbolic capital of the nobility (honor, reputation), which hitherto rested on social esteem tacitly accorded on the basis of a more or less conscious social consensus, now finds a quasi-bureaucratic statutory objectification (in the form of edicts and rulings that do little more than record the new consensus). We find an indication of this in the "grand researches of nobility" undertaken by Louis XIV and Colbert: the decree (*arrêt*) of March 22, 1666, stipulates the creation of a "registry containing the names, surnames, residences and arms of real gentlemen." The intendants scrutinize the titles of nobility, and genealogists of the Orders of the King and *juges d'armes* fight over the definition of true nobles. With the *noblesse de robe*, which owes its position to its cultural capital, we come very close to the logic of state nomination and to the *cursus honorum* founded upon educational credentials.

In short, there is a shift from a diffuse symbolic capital, resting solely on collective recognition, to an *objectified symbolic capital,* codified, delegated and guaranteed by the state, in a word *bureau-cratized*. One finds a very precise illustration of this process in the sumptuary laws intended to regulate, in a rigorously hierarchized manner, the distribution of symbolic expressions (in terms of dress, in particular) between noblemen and commoners and especially perhaps among the different ranks of the nobility.[26] Thus the state regulates the use of cloth and of trimmings of gold, silver, and silk. By doing this, it defends the nobility against the usurpation of commoners but, at the same time, it expands and reinforces its own control over hierarchy within the nobility.

The decline of the power of autonomous distribution of the great lords tends to grant the king the monopoly of ennoblement and the monopoly over *nomination* through the progressive trans-formation of offices – conceived as rewards – into positions of responsibilities requiring competency and participation in a *cursus honorum* that foreshadows a bureaucratic career ladder. Thus, that supremely mysterious power that is the power of *appointing and dismissing the high officers of the state* is slowly instituted. The state is thus constituted as "fountain of honour, of office and privilege," to recall Blackstone's words, and distributes honors. It dubs "knights" and "baronets," invents new orders of knight-hood, confers ceremonial precedence and nominates peers and all the holders of important public functions.[27]

Nomination is, when we stop to think of it, a very mysterious act which follows a logic quite similar to that of magic as described by Marcel Mauss.[28] Just as the sorcerer mobilizes the capital of belief accumulated by the functioning of the magical universe, the President of the Republic who signs a decree of nomination or the physician who signs a certificate (of illness, invalidity, etc.) mobil-izes a symbolic capital accumulated in and through the whole net-work of relations of recognition constitutive of the bureaucratic universe. Who certifies the validity of the certificate? It is the one who signs the credential giving license to certify. But who then certifies this? We are carried through an infinite regression at the end of which "one has to stop" and where one could, following medieval theologians, choose to give the name of "state" to the last (or to the first) link in the long chain of official acts of con-secration.[29] It is the state, acting in the manner of a bank of sym-bolic capital, that guarantees all acts of authority – acts at once arbitrary and misrecognized as such (Austin called them "acts of

legitimate imposture").[30] The president of the country is someone
who claims to be the president but who differs from the madman
who claims to be Napoleon by the fact that he is recognized as
founded to do so.

The nomination or the certificate belongs to the category of
official acts or discourses, symbolically effective only because they
are accomplished in a situation of authority by authorized characters, "officials" who are acting *ex officio*, as holders of an *officium*
(*publicum*), that is, of a function or position assigned by the state.
The sentence of the judge or the grade of the professor, the procedures of official registration, certified reports or minutes, all the
acts meant to carry legal effect, such as certificates of birth, marriage, or death, etc., all manners of public summons as performed
with the required formalities by the appropriate agents (judges,
notaries, bailiffs, officers of *état civil*) and duly registered in the
appropriate office, all these facts invoke the logic of official nomination to institute socially guaranteed identities (as citizen, legal
resident, voter, taxpayer, parent, property owner) as well as legitimate unions and groupings (families, associations, trade unions,
parties, etc.). By stating with authority what a being (thing or
person) is in truth (verdict) according to its socially legitimate
definition, that is, what he or she is authorized to be, what they
have a right (and duty) to be, the social being that they may claim,
the state wields a genuinely *creative*, quasi-divine, power. It suffices
to think of the kind of immortality that it can grant through acts
of consecration such as commemorations or scholarly canoniza-
tion, to see how, twisting Hegel's famous expression, we may say
that "the judgment of the state is the last judgment."[31]

Minds of State

In order truly to understand the power of the state in its full
specificity, that is, the particular symbolic efficacy it wields, one
must, as I suggested long ago in another article,[32] integrate into
one and the same explanatory model intellectual traditions cus-
tomarily perceived as incompatible. It is necessary, first, to over-
come the opposition between a physicalist vision of the social
world that conceives of social relations as relations of physical force
and a "cybernetic" or semiological vision which portrays them as

relations of symbolic force, as relations of meaning or relations of communication. The most brutal relations of force are always simultaneously symbolic relations. And acts of submission and obedience are cognitive acts which as such involve cognitive structures, forms and categories of perception, principles of vision and division. Social agents construct the social world through cognitive structures that may be applied to all things of the world and in particular to social structures (Cassirer called these principles of vision and division "symbolic forms" and Durkheim "forms of classification": these are so many ways of saying the same thing in more or less separate theoretical traditions).

These cognitive structures are historically constituted forms and therefore arbitrary in the Saussurean sense, conventional, *ex instituto*, as Leibniz said, which means that we can trace their social genesis. Generalizing the Durkheimian hypothesis according to which the "forms of classification" that the "primitives" apply to the world are the product of the embodiment of their group structures, we may seek the basis of these cognitive structures in the actions of the state. Indeed, we may posit that, in differentiated societies, the state has the ability to impose and inculcate in a universal manner, within a given territorial expanse, a *nomos*, a shared principle of vision and division, identical or similar cognitive and evaluative structures. And that the state is therefore the foundation of a "logical conformism" and of a "moral conformism" (these are Durkheim's expressions),[33] of a tacit, prereflexive agreement over the meaning of the world which itself lies at the basis of the experience of the world as "commonsense world." (Neither the phenomenologists, who brought this experience to light, nor the ethnomethodologists, who assign themselves the task of describing it, have the means of accounting for this experience because they fail to raise the question of the social construction of the principles of construction of the social reality that they strive to explicate and to question the contribution of the state to the constitution of the principles of constitution that agents apply to the social order.)

In less differentiated societies, the common principles of vision and division – the paradigm of which is the opposition masculine/feminine – are instituted in minds (or in bodies) through the whole spatial and temporal organization of social life, and especially through *rites of institution* that establish definite differences

between those who submitted to the rite and those who did not.[34]
In our societies, the state makes a decisive contribution to the production and reproduction of the instruments of construction of
social reality. As organizational structure and regulator of practices,
the state exerts an ongoing action formative of durable dispositions
through the whole range of constraints and through the corporeal
and mental discipline it uniformly imposes upon all agents. Furthermore, it imposes and inculcates all the fundamental principles
of classification, based on sex, age, "skill," etc. And it lies at the
basis of the symbolic efficacy of all rites of institution, such as
those underlying the family for example, or those that operate
through the routine functioning of the school system as the site of
consecration where lasting and often irrevocable differences are
instituted between the chosen and the excluded, in the manner of
the medieval ritual of the dubbing of knights.

The construction of the state is accompanied by the construction of a sort of common historical transcendental, immanent to
all its "subjects." Through the framing it imposes upon practices,
the state establishes and inculcates common forms and categories
of perception and appreciation, social frameworks of perceptions,
of understanding or of memory, in short *state forms of classification*. It thereby creates the conditions for a kind of immediate
orchestration of habitus which is itself the foundation of a consensus over this set of shared evidences constitutive of (national)
common sense. Thus, for example, the great rhythms of the societal
calendar (think of the schedule of school or patriotic vacations
that determine the great "seasonal migrations" of many contemporary societies) provide both shared objective referents and compatible subjective principles of division which underlie internal
experiences of time sufficiently concordant to make social life
possible.[35]

But in order fully to understand the immediate submission that
the state order elicits, it is necessary to break with the intellectualism of the neo-Kantian tradition to acknowledge that cognitive structures are not forms of consciousness but *dispositions of
the body*. That the obedience we grant to the injunctions of the
state cannot be understood either as mechanical submission to an
external force or as conscious consent to an order (in the double
sense of the term). The social world is riddled with *calls to order*
that function as such only for those who are predisposed to heeding

them as they *awaken* deeply buried corporeal dispositions, out-side the channels of consciousness and calculation. It is this doxic submission of the dominated to the structures of a social order of which their mental structures are the product that Marxism can-not understand insofar as it remains trapped in the intellectualist tradition of the philosophies of consciousness. In the notion of false consciousness that it invokes to account for effects of sym-bolic domination, the superfluous term is "consciousness." And to speak of "ideologies" is to locate in the realm of *representations* – liable to be transformed through this intellectual conversion called "awakening of consciousness" (*prise de conscience*) – what in fact belongs to the order of *belief*, that is, to the level of the most profound corporeal dispositions. Submission to the estab-lished order is the product of the agreement between, on the one hand, the cognitive structures inscribed in bodies by both col-lective history (phylogenesis) and individual history (ontogenesis) and, on the other, the objective structures of the world to which these cognitive structures are applied. State injunctions owe their obviousness, and thus their potency, to the fact that the state has imposed the very cognitive structures through which it is perceived (one should rethink along those lines the conditions that make possible the supreme sacrifice: *pro patria mori*).

But we need to go beyond the neo-Kantian tradition, even in its Durkheimian form, on yet another count. Because it focuses on the *opus operatum*, symbolic structuralism à la Lévi-Strauss (or the Foucault of *The Order of Things*) is bound to neglect the active dimension of symbolic production (as, for example, with mythologies), the question of the *modus operandi*. It does have the advantage of seeking to uncover the internal coherence of sym-bolic systems *qua* systems, that is, one of the major bases of their efficacy – as can be clearly seen in the case of the law, in which coherence is deliberately sought, but also in myth and religion. Symbolic order rests on the imposition upon all agents of struc-turing structures that owe part of their consistency and resilience to the fact that they are coherent and systematic (at least in appear-ance) and that they are objectively in agreement with the objective structures of the social world. It is this immediate and tacit agree-ment, in every respect opposed to an explicit contract, that founds the relation of *doxic submission* which attaches us to the estab-lished order with all the ties of the unconscious. The recognition

of legitimacy is not, as Weber believed, a free act of clear conscience. It is rooted in the immediate, prereflexive agreement between
objective structures and embodied structures, now turned unconscious (such as those that organize temporal rhythms: for instance,
the quite arbitrary divisions of schooltime into periods).

It is this prereflexive agreement that explains the ease, rather
stunning when we think of it, with which the dominant impose
their domination:

> Nothing is as astonishing for those who consider human affairs
> with a philosophic eye than to see the ease with which the *many*
> will be governed by the *few* and to observe the implicit submission
> with which men revoke their own sentiments and passions in favor
> of their leaders. When we inquire about the means through which
> such an astonishing thing is accomplished, we find that force being
> always on the side of the governed, only opinion can sustain the
> governors. It is thus solely on opinion that government is founded,
> and such maxim applies to the most despotic and military govern-
> ment as well as to the freest and most popular.[36]

Hume's astonishment brings forth the fundamental question of
all political philosophy, which one occults, paradoxically, by posing
a problem that is not really posed as such in ordinary existence:
the problem of legitimacy. Indeed, essentially, what is problematic is the fact that the established order is *not* problematic; and
that the question of the legitimacy of the state, and of the order it
institutes, does not arise except in crisis situations. The state does
not necessarily have to give orders or to exercise physical coercion in order to produce an ordered social world, as long as it is
capable of producing embodied cognitive structures that accord
with objective structures and thus of ensuring the belief of which
Hume spoke – namely, doxic submission to the established order.

This being said, it should not be forgotten that such primordial
political belief, this doxa, is an orthodoxy, a right, correct, dominant vision which has more often than not been imposed through
struggles against competing visions. This means that the "natural
attitude" mentioned by the phenomenologists, that is, the primary
experience of the world of common sense, is a politically produced
relation, as are the categories of perception that sustain it. What
appears to us today as self-evident, as beneath consciousness and

choice, has quite often been the stake of struggles and instituted only as the result of dogged confrontations between dominant and dominated groups. The major effect of historical evolution is to abolish history by relegating to the past, that is, to the unconscious, the lateral possibles that it eliminated. The analysis of the genesis of the state as the foundation of the principles of vision and division operative within its territorial expanse enables us to understand at once the doxic adherence to the order established by the state and also the properly political foundations of such apparently natural adherence. Doxa is a particular point of view, the point of view of the dominant, which presents and imposes itself as a universal point of view – the point of view of those who dominate by dominating the state and who have constituted their point of view as universal by constituting the state.

Thus, to account fully for the properly symbolic dimension of the power of the state, we may build on Max Weber's decisive contribution (in his writings on religion) to the theory of symbolic systems by reintroducing specialized agents and their specific interests. Indeed, if he shares with Marx an interest in the function – rather than the structure – of symbolic systems, Weber nonetheless has the merit of calling attention to the producers of these particular products (religious agents, in the case that concerns him) and to their *interactions* (conflict, competition, etc.).[37] In opposition to the Marxists, who have overlooked the existence of specialized agents of production (notwithstanding a famous text of Engels which states that to understand law one needs to focus on the corporation of the jurists), Weber reminds us that, to understand religion, it does not suffice to study symbolic forms of the religious type, as Cassirer or Durkheim did, or even the immanent structure of the religious message or of the mythological corpus, as with the structuralists. Weber focuses specifically on the producers of the religious message, on the specific interests that move them and on the strategies they use in their struggle (for example, excommunication). In order to grasp these symbolic systems simultaneously in their function, structure and genesis, it suffices, thence, to apply the structuralist mode of thinking (completely alien to Weber) not solely to the symbolic systems or, better, to the space of *position-takings* or stances adopted in a determinate domain of practice (such as religious messages), but to the system of agents who produce them as well or, to be more precise,

to the space of *positions* they occupy (what I call the religious
field) in the competition that opposes them.[38]

The same holds for the state. To understand the symbolic dimension of the effect of the state, and in particular what we may call
the *effect of universality*, it is necessary to understand the specific
functioning of the bureaucratic microcosm and thus to analyze
the genesis and structure of this universe of agents of the state
who have constituted themselves into a state nobility by instituting the state,[39] and in particular by producing the performative
discourse on the state which, under the guise of saying what the
state is, caused the state to come into being by stating what it
should be – that is, what should be the position of the producers
of this discourse in the division of labor of domination. One
must focus in particular on the structure of the juridical field and
uncover both the generic interests of the holders of that particular form of cultural capital, predisposed to function as symbolic
capital, that is juridical competence, as well as the specific interests imposed on each of them by virtue of their position in a
juridical field still only weakly autonomous (that is, in essence, in
relation to royal power). And to account for those effects of
universality and rationality I just evoked, it is necessary to understand why these agents had an interest in giving a universal form
to the expression of their vested interests, in elaborating a theory
of public service and of public order, and thus in working to
autonomize the *reason of state* from dynastic reason, from the
"house of the king," and to invent thereby the "res publica" and
later the republic as an instance transcendent to the agents (the
king included) who are its temporary incarnations. One must
understand how, by virtue and because of their specific capital
and particular interests, they were led to produce a discourse of
state which, by providing justifications for their own positions,
constituted the state: this *fictio juris* which slowly stopped being
a mere fiction of jurists to become an autonomous order capable
of imposing ever more widely the submission to its functions and
to its functioning and the recognition of its principles.

The Monopolization of Monopoly

The construction of the state monopoly over physical and symbolic violence is inseparable from the construction of the field of

struggles for the monopoly over the advantages attached to this monopoly. The relative unification and universalization associated with the emergence of the state has for counterpart the monopolization by the few of the universal resources that it produces and procures (Weber, and Elias after him, ignored the process of constitution of a statist capital and the process of monopolization of this capital by the state nobility which has contributed to its production or, better, which has produced itself as such by producing it). However, this *monopoly of the universal* can only be obtained at the cost of a submission (if only in appearance) to the universal and of a universal recognition of the universalist representation of domination presented as legitimate and disinterested. Those who – like Marx – invert the official image that the bureaucracy likes to give of itself, and describe bureaucrats as usurpers of the universal who act as private proprietors of public resources, ignore the very real effects of the obligatory reference to the values of neutrality and disinterested loyalty to the public good. Such values impose themselves with increasing force upon the functionaries of the state as the history of the long work of symbolic construction unfolds whereby the official representation of the state as the site of universality and of service to the general interest is invented and imposed.

The monopolization of the universal is the result of a work of universalization which is accomplished within the bureaucratic field itself. As would be revealed by the analysis of the functioning of this strange institution called a *commission*, that is, a set of individuals vested with a mission of general interest and invited to transcend their particular interests in order to produce universal propositions, officials constantly have to labor, if not to sacrifice their particular point of view on behalf of the "point of view of society," at least to constitute their point of view into a legitimate one, that is, as universal, especially through use of the rhetoric of the official.

The universal is the object of universal recognition and the sacrifice of selfish (especially economic) interests is universally recognized as legitimate. (In the effort to rise from the singular and selfish point of view of the individual to the point of view of the group, collective judgment cannot but perceive, and approve, an expression of recognition of the value of the group and of the group itself as the fount of all value, and thus a passage from "is" to "ought".) This means that all social universes tend to offer, to varying degrees, material or symbolic profits of universalization (those very profits pursued by strategies seeking to "play by the rule"). It also implies that the universes which, like the bureaucratic field, demand with the utmost insistence that one submits to the universal, are particularly favorable to obtaining such profits.

The profit of universalization is undoubtedly one of the historical engines of the progress of the universal. This is because it favors the creation of universes where universal values (reason, virtue, etc.) are at least verbally recognized and wherein operates a circular process of mutual reinforcement of the strategies of universalization seeking to obtain the profits (if only negative) associated with conformity to universal rules and to the structures of those universes officially devoted to the universal. The sociological vision cannot ignore the discrepancy between the official norm as stipulated in administrative law and the reality of bureaucratic practice, with all its violations of the obligation of disinterestedness, all the cases of "private use of public services" (from the diversion of public goods and functions to graft to corruption). Nor can it ignore the more perverse abuses of law and the administrative tolerances, exemptions, bartering of favors that result from the faulty implementation or from the transgression of the law. Yet sociology cannot for all that remain blind to the effects of this norm which demands that agents sacrifice their private interests for the obligations inscribed in their function ("the agent should devote himself fully to his function"), or, in a more realistic manner, to the effects of the interest attached to disinterestedness and of all those forms of "pious hypocrisy" that the paradoxical logic of the bureaucratic field can promote.

Notes

1 Thomas Bernhard, *The Old Masters*, trans. Ewald Osers (London: Quartet, 1989), p. 27.
2 Institut National de la Statistique et des Études Économiques (National Institute of Statistics and Economic Studies).
3 Pierre Bourdieu, *Language and Symbolic Power* (Cambridge: Polity Press, 1991), ch. 2.

4 Émile Durkheim, *Leçons de sociologie* (Paris: PUF, 1922), esp. pp. 84–90.

5 Richard Bonney, "Guerre, fiscalité et activité d'État en France (1500–1660): quelques remarques preliminaires sur les possibilités de recherche," in P. Genet and M. Le Mené (eds), *Genèse de l'État moderne. Prélèvement et redistribution* (Paris: CNRS, 1987), pp. 193–201, at p. 193.

6 e.g. Charles Tilly, *Coercion, Capital, and European States, AD 990–1990* (Oxford: Blackwell, 1990), esp. ch. 3.

7 See N. Elias, *State Formation and Civilization* (Oxford: Blackwell, 1982) and *The Civilizing Process* (Oxford: Blackwell, 1978).

8 In societies without a state, such as ancient Kabylia or the Iceland of the sagas (see William Ian Miller, *Bloodtaking and Peacemaking* (Chicago: University of Chicago Press, 1990), there is no delegation of the exercise of violence to a specialized group, clearly identified as such within society. It follows that one cannot escape the logic of personal revenge (to take justice into one's hands, *rekba* or *vendetta*) or of self-defense. Thus the question raised by the Tragedies: is not the act of the justice-maker Orestes a crime just as the initial act of the criminal was? This is a question eliminated by recognition of the legitimacy of the state so that it reappears only in very specific and extreme situations.

9 One would have to analyze the progressive shift from a "patrimonial" (or feudal) usage of fiscal resources where a major part of the public revenue is expended in gifts and in generosities destined to ensure the Prince the recognition of potential competitors (and therefore, among other things, the recognition of the legitimacy of fiscal levies) to a "bureaucratic" usage of such resources as "public expenditures." This shift is one of the most fundamental dimensions of the transformation of the dynastic state into the "impersonal," bureaucratic state.

10 See J. Dubergé, *La psychologie sociale de l'impôt* (Paris: PUF, 1961), and G. Schmolders, *Psychologie des finances et de l'impôt* (Paris: PUF, 1973).

11 Rodney H. Hilton, "Resistance to Taxation and Other State Impositions in Medieval England," in Genet and Le Mené, *Genèse de l'État moderne*, pp. 167–77, esp. pp. 173–4.

12 This disjunction of the king or the state from concrete incarnations of power finds its fullest expression in the myth of the "hidden king," see Y. M. Bercé, *Le Roi caché* (Paris: Fayard, 1991).

13 Y.-M. Bercé, "Pour une étude institutionnelle et psychologique de l'impôt moderne," in Genet and Le Mené, *Genèse de l'État moderne*.

14 The ideal of feudal princes, as well as of the kings of France later, was to allow only the use of their own money within the territories they dominated – an ideal only realized under Louis XIV.

15 "Culture" is capitalized in the French original to mark the appropriation of the emerging bodies of knowledge linked to the state by the dominant, i.e., the emergence of a dominant culture. *Trans.*

16 It is especially through the school, with the generalization of elementary education through the nineteenth century, that the unifying action of the state is exercised in matters of culture. (This is a fundamental component in the construction of the nation-state.) The creation of national society goes hand in hand with universal educability: the fact that all individuals are equal before the law gives the state the duty of turning them into citizens, endowed with the cultural means actively to exercise their civic rights.

17 P. Corrigan and D. Sayer, *The Great Arch: English State Formation as Cultural Revolution* (Oxford: Blackwell, 1985), p. 103.

18 See Pierre Bourdieu, "Deux impérialismes de l'universel," in C. Fauré and T. Bishop (eds), *L'Amérique des français* (Paris: François Bourin, 1992), pp. 149–55. Culture is so intimately bound up with patriotic symbols that any critical questioning of its functions and functioning tends to be perceived as *treason* and sacrilege.

19 Pierre Bourdieu, "The Sentiment of Honour in Kabyle Society," in J. G. Peristiany (ed.), *Honour and Shame: the Values of Mediterranean Society* (London: Weidenfeld and Nicholson, 1965), pp. 191–241.

20 See A. Esmein, *Histoire de la procédure criminelle en France et spécialement de la procédure inquisitoire depuis le XIIe siècle jusqu' à nos jours* (1882; Frankfurt: Sauer and Auvermann, 1969). See also H. J. Berman, *Law and Revolution: the Formation of the Western Legal Tradition* (Cambridge: Harvard University Press, 1983).

21 Marc Bloch, *Seigneurie française et manoir anglais* (Paris: A. Colin, 1967), p. 85.

22 The functioning of this field is sketched in Pierre Bourdieu, "The Force of Law: Towards a Sociology of the Juridical Field," *Hastings Journal of Law* 38 (1987), pp. 209–48.

23 S. Hanley, "Engendering the State: Family Formation and State Building in Early Modern France," *French Historical Studies* 16, no. 1 (spring 1989), pp. 4–27.

24 A. Jouanna, *Le devoir de révolte. La noblesse française et la gestation de l'État moderne, 1559–1561* (Paris: Fayard, 1989).

25 R. Mousnier, *Les institutions de la France sous la monarchie absolue* (Paris: PUF, 1980), p. 94.

26 Michel Fogel, "Modèle d'État et modèle social de dépense: les lois somptuaires en France de 1485 à 1560," in Genet and Le Mené, *Genèse de l'État moderne*, pp. 227–35, esp. p. 232.

27 F. W. Maitland, *The Constitutional History of England* (Cambridge: Cambridge University Press, 1948), p. 429.

28 M. Mauss, *A General Theory of Magic* (1902–3; New York: Norton, 1975).

29 Using Kafka, I have shown how the sociological vision and the theological vision meet in spite of their apparent opposition (see Pierre Bourdieu, "La dernière instance," in *Le siècle de Kafka* (Paris: Centre Georges Pompidou, 1984), pp. 268–70.

30 John Austin, *How to Do Things with Words* (Oxford: Oxford University Press, 1952).

31 Publication, in the sense of a procedure aimed at rendering a state or act public, at bringing it to everybody's knowledge, always holds the potentiality of a usurpation of the right to exercise the symbolic violence which properly belongs to the state (and which is expressed, for example, in the publication of marriage notices or the promulgation of law). Hence, the state always tends to regulate all forms of publication, printing, theatrical performances, public preaching, caricature, etc.

32 Pierre Bourdieu, "On Symbolic Power," in *Language and Symbolic Power*, pp. 163–70 (originally in *Annales* 3 (June 1977), pp. 405–11).

33 Émile Durkheim, *The Elementary Forms of the Religious Life* (1912; New York: Free Press, 1965).

34 Pierre Bourdieu, "Rites of Institution" (1982), in *Language and Symbolic Power*, pp. 117–26.

35 Another example would be the division of the academic and scientific worlds into disciplines, which is inscribed in minds in the form of disciplinary habitus generating distorted relations between the representatives of different disciplines as well as limitations and mutilations in the representations and practices of each of them.

36 David Hume. "On the First Principles of Government," in *Essays and Treatises on Several Subjects*, 1758.

37 For a fuller discussion, see Pierre Bourdieu, "Legitimation and Structured Interests in Weber's Sociology of Religion," in Sam Whimster and Scott Lash (eds), *Max Weber, Rationality and Modernity* (London: Allen and Unwin, 1987), pp. 119–36.

38 For a fuller demonstration of this point, see Pierre Bourdieu, "Genesis and Structure of the Religious Field" (1971), *Comparative Social Research*, 13 (1991), pp. 1–43.

39 Pierre Bourdieu, *The State Nobility* (Cambridge: Polity Press, 1996), esp. part 5.

APPENDIX

The Family Spirit

The dominant, legitimate definition of the normal family (which may be explicit, as it is in law, or implicit, in for example the family questionnaires used by state statistical agencies) is based on a constellation of words – house, home, household, *maison, maisonnée* – which, while seeming to describe social reality, in fact construct it. On this definition, the family is a set of related individuals linked either by alliance (marriage) or filiation, or, less commonly, by adoption (legal relationship), and living under the same roof (cohabitation). Some ethnomethodologists even go so far as to say that what we regard as a reality is a fiction, constructed to a large extent by the vocabulary that the social world provides us with in order to describe it. Appealing to the "real world" (which, from their own standpoint, is not unproblematic), they point out that a number of the groups that are called "families" in the present-day United States have absolutely no resemblance to this dominant definition, and that in most modern societies the nuclear family is a minority experience compared to the number of unmarried couples living together, single-parent families, married couples living apart, etc.[1] The increase in the rate of cohabitation outside of marriage and the new forms of family bonds that are being invented[2] before our eyes remind us that this family, which we are led to regard as *natural* because it presents itself with the self-evidence of what "has always been that way," is a recent invention (as is shown in particular by the work of Philippe Ariès and Michael Anderson on the genesis of private life or Edward

Shorter on the invention of family feeling), and is perhaps fast disappearing.

But if it is accepted that the family is only a word, a mere verbal construct, one then has to analyze the representations that people form of what they refer to as the family, of this "word family" or "paper family." Some ethnomethodologists who see discourse about the family as a kind of political ideology designating a valorized configuration of social relationships have identified a number of presuppositions common to this discourse in both its ordinary and scientific forms.

First set of properties: through a kind of anthropomorphism in which the properties of an individual are attributed to a group, the family is seen as a reality transcending its members, a transpersonal person endowed with a common life and spirit and a particular vision of the world.

Second set of properties: definitions of the family are seen as having in common the fact that they assume the family exists as a separate social universe, engaged in an effort to perpetuate its frontiers and oriented toward idealization of the interior as sacred, *sanctum* (as opposed to the exterior). This sacred, secret universe, with its doors closed to protect its intimacy, separated from the external world by the symbolic barrier of the threshold, perpetuates itself and perpetuates its own separateness, its *privacy*, as an obstacle to knowledge, a private secret, "backstage." One might add to this theme of privacy a third theme, that of the *residence*, the house as a stable, enduring locus and the household as a permanent unit, durably associated with a house that is endlessly transmissible.

Thus, in *family discourse*, the language that the family uses about the family, the domestic unit is conceived as an active agent, endowed with a will, capable of thought, feeling and action, and founded on a set of cognitive presuppositions and normative prescriptions about the proper way to conduct domestic relationships. It is a world in which the ordinary laws of the economy are suspended, a place of trusting and giving – as opposed to the market and its exchanges of equivalent values – or, to use Aristotle's term, *philia*, a word that is often translated as "friendship" but which in fact designates the refusal to calculate; a place where interest, in the narrow sense of the pursuit of equivalence in exchanges, is suspended. Ordinary discourse ordinarily, and no doubt universally, draws from the family ideal models of human relations (with, for example, concepts like brotherhood), and family relations in their official definition tend to function as principles for the construction and evaluation of every social relationship.

A Well-Founded Fiction

At the same time, if it is true that the family is only a word, it is also true that it is an active "watchword," or rather, a category, a collective principle of construction of collective reality. It can be said without contradiction both that social realities are social fictions with no other basis than social construction, and that they really exist, inasmuch as they are collectively recognized. Every time we use a classificatory concept like "family," we are making both a description and a prescription, which is not perceived as such because it is (more or less) universally accepted and goes without saying. We tacitly admit that the reality to which we give the name "family," and which we place in the category of "real" families, is a family in reality.

So, while we may accept, with the ethnomethodologists, that the family is a principle of construction of social reality, it also has to be pointed out, in opposition to ethnomethodology, that this principle of construction is itself socially constructed and that it is common to all agents socialized in a particular way. In other words, it is a common principle of vision and division, a *nomos*, that we all have in our heads because it has been inculcated in us through a process of socialization performed in a world that was itself organized according to the division into families. This principle of construction is one of the constituent elements of our habitus, a mental structure which, having been inculcated into all minds socialized in a particular way, is both individual and collective. It is a tacit law (*nomos*) of perception and practice that is at the basis of the consensus on the sense of the social world (and of the word "family" in particular), the basis of *common sense*. Thus the prenotions of common sense and the folk categories of spontaneous sociology which, methodologically speaking, have to be called into question, may, as here, be well founded, because they help to *make* the reality that they describe. In the social world, words make things, because they make the consensus on the existence and the meaning of things, the common sense, the *doxa* accepted by all as self-evident.[3]

The family is a principle of construction that is both immanent in individuals (as an internalized collective) and transcendent to them, since they encounter it in the form of objectivity in all other individuals; it is a transcendental in Kant's sense, but one which, being immanent in all habitus, imposes itself as transcendent. This is the basis of the specific ontology of social categories: being rooted both in the objectivity of social structures and in the subjectivity of objectively orchestrated mental structures, they present themselves to experience with the opacity and resistance of things, although they are the product of acts of construction which, as a certain ethnomethodological critique suggests, apparently relegate them to the nonexistence of pure figments of thought.

Thus the family as an objective social category (a structuring structure) is the basis of the family as a subjective social category (a structured structure), a mental category which is the matrix of countless representations and actions (such as marriages) which help to reproduce the objective social category. The circle is that of reproduction of the social order. The near-perfect match that is then set up between the subjective and objective categories provides the foundation for an experience of the world as self-evident, taken for granted. And nothing seems more natural than the family; this arbitrary social construct seems to belong on the side of nature, the natural and the universal.

The Work of Institution

If the family appears as the most natural of social categories and is therefore destined to provide the model for all *social bodies*, this is because it functions, in habitus, as a classificatory scheme and a principle of the construction of the social world and of that particular social body, the family, a principle which is acquired within a family existing as a realized social fiction.[4] The family is the product of an *institutionalization*, both ritual and technical, aimed at durably instituting in each member of the instituted unit feelings that will tend to ensure the *integration* that is the condition of the existence and persistence of the unit. Rites of institution (from *stare*, to stand, be stable) aim to constitute the family by establishing it as a united, integrated entity which is therefore stable, constant, indifferent to the fluctuations of individual feelings. And these inaugural acts of creation (imposition of the family name, marriage, etc.) have their logical extension in the countless acts of reaffirmation and reinforcement that aim to produce, in a kind of continuous creation, the *obliged affections* and *affective obligations* of family feeling (conjugal love, paternal and maternal love, filial love, brotherly and sisterly love, etc.). This constant work on the maintenance of feelings complements the performative effect of the simple *naming* which constructs an affective object and socializes the libido (for example, the proposition "she's your sister" contains the imposition of brotherly love as desexualized social libido – the incest taboo).

To understand how the family turns from a nominal fiction into a real group whose members are united by intense affective bonds, one has to take account of all the practical and symbolic work that transforms the obligation to love into a loving disposition and tends to endow each member of the family with a "family feeling" that generates devotion, generosity, and solidarity. This means both the countless ordinary and continuous exchanges of daily existence – exchange of gifts, service, assistance, visits, attention, kindnesses – and the extraordinary and solemn exchanges of family occasions, often sanctioned and memorialized by photographs consecrating the integration of the assembled family. This work falls more particularly to the women, who are responsible for maintaining relationships (not only with their own family but very often also with the spouse's) through visits, correspondence (especially the ritual exchange of good wishes) and, as an American study has shown, telephone calls. The structures of kinship and family as *bodies* can be perpetuated only through a continuous creation of family feeling, a cognitive principle of vision and division that is at the same time an affective principle of *cohesion*, that is, the adhesion that is vital to the existence of a family group and its interests.

This work of integration is all the more necessary since the family – while being obliged to assert itself as a *body* in order to exist and persist – still tends to function as a *field*, with its physical, economic and, above all, symbolic power relations (linked, for example, to the volume and structure of the capital possessed by each member), and its struggles to hold on to and transform these power relations.

The Site of Social Reproduction

But the naturalization of social arbitrariness causes it to be forgotten that, in order for this reality called "family" to be possible, certain social conditions that are in no way universal have to be fulfilled. They are, in any case, by no means uniformly distributed. In short, the family in its legitimate definition is a privilege instituted into a universal norm: a de facto privilege that implies a symbolic privilege – the privilege of being *comme il faut*, conforming to the norm, and therefore enjoying a symbolic profit of normality. Those who have the privilege of having a "normal" family are able to demand the same of everyone without having to raise the question of the conditions (a certain income, living space, etc.) of universal access to what they demand universally.

This privilege is, in reality, one of the major conditions of the accumulation and transmission of economic, cultural and symbolic privileges. The family plays a decisive role in the maintenance of the social order, through social as well as biological reproduction, that is, reproduction of the structure of the social space and social relations. It is one of the key sites of the accumulation of capital in its different forms, and its transmission between the generations. It safeguards its unity for and through this transmission. It is the main "subject" of reproduction strategies. That is seen clearly in the transmission of the *family name*, the basic element in the hereditary symbolic capital. The father is only the apparent subject of the naming of his son because he names him in accordance with a principle of which he is not the master, and in transmitting his own name (the *name of the father*) he transmits an *auctoritas* of which he is not the *auctor*, according to a rule of which he is not the creator. The same is true, *mutatis mutandis*, of the material heritage. A considerable number of economic acts have as their "subject" not the individual *homo economicus* but collectives, one of the most important of these being the family; this is as true of the choice of a school as of the purchase of a house. For example, in property purchases the decision often involves a large part of the lineage (such as the parents of one or the other of the spouses, who lend money and in turn have the right to give advice and influence the economic decision). It is true that, in this case, the family acts as a kind of "collective subject," as commonly defined, and not as a simple aggregate of individuals. But this is not the only case in which it is the site of a kind of transcendent will manifesting itself in collective decisions and in which its members feel required to act as parts of a united body.

At the same time, not all families, and, within a given family, not all members, have the same capacity and propensity to conform to the dominant definition. As is seen especially clearly in societies based on the "house," where the perpetuation of the house as a set of material assets orients the whole existence of the household,[5] the tendency of the family to persevere in its being, to perpetuate its existence by ensuring its integration, is inseparable from the tendency to perpetuate the integrity of its heritage, which is always threatened by dilapidation and dispersion. The forces of fusion, especially the ethical dispositions that incline its members to identify the particular interests of individuals with the collective interests of the family, have to contain the forces of fission, that is, the interests of the various members of the group, who may be more or less inclined to accept the common vision and more or less capable of imposing their "selfish" point of view. The practices of which the family is the "subject" (for instance, "choices" as regards fertility, child-rearing and education, marriage, consumption) cannot be accounted for without considering the structure of the power relations among the members of the family group (and therefore the history of which it is the outcome), a structure that is always at stake in the struggles within the domestic field. But the functioning of the domestic unit as a *field* meets its limit in the effects of male domination, which orient the family toward the logic of the monolithic *body* (since integration can be an effect of domination).

One of the properties of dominant social fractions is that they have particularly extensive families ("great" families are big families) that are strongly integrated because they are united not only by the affinity between habitus but also by the solidarity of interests, that is, both by capital and for capital, economic capital naturally, but also symbolic capital (the name) and perhaps above all social capital (which can be shown to be the condition and the effect of successful management of the capital collectively possessed by the members of the domestic unit). For example, among executives, the family plays a considerable role not only in the transmission but also in the management of the economic heritage, especially through business alliances which are often family alliances. Bourgeois dynasties function like select clubs; they are the sites of the accumulation and management of a capital equal to the sum of the capital held by each of their members, the relationships between the various holders making it possible to mobilize it, partially at least, in favor of each of them.

The State and the Statisticians

Thus, having started out with a form of radical doubt, we are led to retain a number of the properties that figure in the ordinary definitions; but only after subjecting them to a twofold challenge that only apparently leads back to the starting point. Undoubtedly one has to cease to regard the family as an immediate datum of social reality and see it rather as an instrument of construction of that reality; but one also has to move beyond the ethnomethodological challenge and ask who constructed the instruments of construction that are thereby brought to light, and to examine family categories as institutions existing both in the objectivity of the world, in the form of the elementary social bodies that we call families, and in people's minds, in the form of principles of classification that are implemented both by ordinary agents and by the licensed operators of official classifications, such as state statisticians (working for INED, INSEE,[6] etc.).

It is indeed clear that in modern societies the main agent of the *construction of the official categories* through which both populations and minds are structured is the state, which, through a whole labor of codification accompanied by economic and social effects (family allowances, for example), aims to favor a certain kind of family organization, to strengthen those who are in a position to conform to this form of organization, and to encourage, through all material and symbolic means, "logical conformism" and "moral conformism" as an agreement on a system of forms of apprehension and construction of the world, of which this form of organization, this category, is without doubt the cornerstone.

If radical doubt remains indispensable, this is because simple positivistic recording (the family exists, we have met it under our statistical scalpel) is liable to contribute, though the effect of *ratification*, of *registration*, to the construction work on social reality that is implied in the word "family" and in the family talk which, under the appearance of describing a social reality, the family, prescribes a mode of existence: family life. By uncritically implementing state thinking, that is, the thought categories of common sense inculcated by the action of the state, the official statisticians help to reproduce the thinking that is part of the conditions of functioning of the family – a supposedly private reality that is of public origin. The same is true of the judges or social workers who, very spontaneously, when they want to predict the probable effects of a punishment or remission of sentence, or even to evaluate the weight of the punishment given to a young offender, take account of a number of indicators of conformity to the official idea of the family.[7] In a kind of circle, the native category, having become a scientific category for demographers, sociologists and especially social workers who, like official statisticians, are invested with the capacity to work on reality, to make reality, helps to give real existence to that category. The *family discourse* that ethnomethodologists refer to is an *institutional discourse* that is powerful and performative and which has the means of creating the conditions of its own verification and therefore its own reinforcement.

The state, through its official recording operations (inscribed in France in the *livret de famille*), performs countless constituting acts which constitute family identity as one of the most powerful principles of perception of the social world and one of the most real social units. A social history of the process of state institutionalization of the family – which would be much more radical than ethnomethodological critique – would show that the traditional opposition between the public and the private conceals the extent to which the public is present in the private, and in the very notion of *privacy*. Being the product of a sustained effort of juridical and political construction culminating in the modern family, the private is a public matter. The public vision (the *nomos*, this time in the sense of *law*) is deeply involved in our vision of domestic things, and our most private behaviors themselves depend on public actions, such as housing policy or, more directly, family policy.[8]

Thus the family is indeed a fiction, a social artifact, an illusion in the most ordinary sense of the word, but a "well-founded illusion," because, being produced and reproduced with the guarantee of the state, it receives from the state at every moment the means to exist and persist.

Appendix Notes

1 I will cite just one work exemplary in its audacious application of ethnomethodological doubt: J. F. Gubrium and J. A. Holstein, *What is Family?* (Mountain View, Calif.: Mayfield, 1990).
2 In the absence of empirical studies, I will cite here, for the case of France, the work of the cartoonist Claire Bretécher, an excellent ethnographer of a very particular social milieu. In one of her books, *Agrippine,* her heroine spells out a whole new taxonomy corresponding to entirely unprecedented kin relationships – "pseudo-half" (brother), "half," "double-half," "half-double" – devised to designate all the forms of kinship made possible by remarriages or (pseudo-)divorces. In short, to understand some of the family combinations really existing today in the social world, one would have to follow Bretécher and construct an entirely new kinship terminology overriding all the structural oppositions that componential analyses of kinship normally bring out.
3 To convey the full force of this shared self-evidence one would need to relate here the testimony of the women we recently interviewed in the course of a survey on social suffering: being out of line with the tacit norm which demands, with increasing insistence as they grow older, that they should be married and have children, they speak of the pressures exerted on them to fall into line, to "settle down" and start a family (such as the harassments and problems associated with the status of single woman, at receptions or dinner parties, or the difficulty of being taken completely seriously when one is seen as an incomplete and inadequate person).
4 Ethnomethodological critique leaves unanswered the question of the genesis of the social categories of construction of social reality, the acquisition of the durable dispositions that constitute the habitus. Similarly it fails to address the question of the social conditions of possibility both of this process of acquisition and of the family as a realized social category.
5 On the "house," see Pierre Bourdieu, "Célibat et condition paysanne," *Études Rurales* 5–6 (Apr.–Sept. 1962), pp. 32–136; "Les stratégies matrimoniales dans le système des stratégies de reproduction," *Annales*

4–5 (July–Oct. 1972), pp. 1105–27; and also, among others, C. Klapisch-Zuber, *La Maison et le Nom* (Paris: École des Hautes Études en Sciences Sociales, 1990).

6 French national institutes for demographic and socioeconomic statistics, respectively. *Trans.*

7 These indicators are often provided by sociologists, as has been shown by an American study of the criteria social workers use to make a rapid assessment of the cohesion of the family. This assessment then provides the basis for a forecast of the chances of success of a given course of action and, consequently, one of the mediations through which social destiny is accomplished.

8 For example, the major commissions that have decided the form that state housing aid should take have made a major contribution toward shaping the family and the representation of family life that demographic and sociological surveys record as a kind of natural datum.

4

Is a Disinterested Act Possible?

W hy is the word interest to a certain point interesting? Why is it important to ask about the interest agents may have in doing what they do? In fact, the notion of interest first imposed itself on me as an *instrument of rupture* with an enchanted and mystifying vision of human behavior. The furor or horror that my work sometimes provokes is perhaps in part explained by the fact that its somewhat disenchanted gaze, while not sniggering or cynical, is often applied to universes, such as the intellectual world, which are sites par excellence of disinterestedness (at least according to the representation of those who participate in them). To recall that intellectual games also have stakes and that these stakes arouse interests – as so many things that everyone in a sense knows – was to attempt to extend the scientific vision's universal mode of explanation and comprehension to all forms of human behavior, including those presented or lived as disinterested, and to remove the intellectual world from the status of an exception or an extraterritoriality that intellectuals are inclined to accord themselves.

As a second justification, I could invoke what seems to me to be a postulate of the sociological theory of knowledge. One cannot do sociology without accepting what classical philosophers called the "principle of sufficient reason" and without assuming, among other things, that social agents don't do just anything, that they are not foolish, that they do not act without reason. This does not mean that one must assume that they are rational, that they are right to act as they do, or even, to put it more simply, that they have reasons to act and that reasons are what direct, guide, or orient their actions. Agents may engage in reasonable forms of behavior without being rational; they may engage in behaviors one can explain, as the classical philosophers would say, with the hypothesis of rationality, without their behavior having reason as its principle. They may conduct themselves in such a way that, starting with a rational evaluation of their chances for success, it seems that they were right in doing what they did, without one being justified in saying that a rational calculation of chances was at the origin of the choices they made.

Sociology thus postulates that there is a reason in what agents do (in the sense that one speaks of a reason of a series) which must be found; this reason permits one to explain and to transform a series of apparently incoherent, arbitrary behaviors into a coherent series, into something that can be understood according to a unique principle or a coherent set of principles. In this sense, sociology postulates that social agents do not engage in gratuitous acts.

The word "gratuitous" refers, on the one hand, to the idea of unmotivated, arbitrary: a gratuitous act is one which cannot be explained (such as that of Gide's Lafcadio), a foolish, absurd act – it matters little – about which social science has nothing to say and in face of which it can only resign. This first sense conceals another, more common meaning: that which is gratuitous is that which is for nothing, is not profitable, costs nothing, is not lucrative. Telescoping these two meanings, the search for the *raison d'être* of a behavior is identified with the explanation of that behavior as the pursuit of economic ends.

Investment

Having defended my usage of the notion of interest, I will now attempt to show how it can be replaced by more rigorous notions such as *illusio, investment,* or even *libido.* In his well-known book, *Homo Ludens,* Huizinga says that through a false etymology, one can make *illusio,* a Latin word derived from the root *ludus* (game), mean the fact of being in the game, of being invested in the game, of taking the game seriously. *Illusio* is the fact of being caught up in and by the game, of believing the game is "worth the candle," or, more simply, that playing is worth the effort. In fact, the word interest initially meant very precisely what I include under the notion of *illusio*, that is, the fact of attributing importance to a social game, the fact that what happens matters to those who are engaged in it, who are in the game. *Interest* is to "be there," to participate, to admit that the game is worth playing and that the stakes created in and through the fact of playing are worth pursuing; it is to recognize the game and to recognize its stakes. When you read, in Saint-Simon, about the quarrel of hats (who should bow first), if you were not born in a court society, if you do not possess the habitus of a person of the court, if the structures of the game are not also in your mind, the quarrel will seem futile and ridiculous to you. If, on the other hand, your mind is structured according to the structures of the world in which you play, everything will seem obvious and the question of knowing if the game is "worth the candle" will not even be asked. In other words, social games are games that are forgotten *qua* games, and the *illusio* is the enchanted relation to a game that is the product of a relation of ontological complicity between mental structures and the objective structures of social space. That is what I meant in speaking of interest: games which matter to you are important and interesting because they have been imposed and introduced in your mind, in your body, in a form called the feel for the game.

The notion of interest is opposed to that of disinterestedness, but also to that of indifference. One can be interested in a game (in the sense of not indifferent), while at the same time being disinterested. The indifferent person "does not see why they are playing," it's all the same to them; they are in the position of Buridan's ass, not making a distinction. Such a person is someone who, not having the principles of vision and division necessary to make distinctions, finds everything the same, is neither moved nor affected. What the Stoics called ataraxia is the soul's indifference, tranquility, or detachment, which is not disinterestedness. *Illusio* is thus the opposite of ataraxia; it is the fact of being invested, of investing in the stakes existing in a certain game, through the effect of competition, and which only exist for people who, being caught up in that game and possessing the dispositions to recognize the stakes at play, are ready to die for the stakes which, conversely, are devoid of interest for those who are not tied to that game and which leave them indifferent. We could thus also use the word *investment* in the double sense of psychoanalysis and of the economy.

Every social field, whether the scientific field, the artistic field, the bureaucratic field, or the political field, tends to require those entering it to have the relationship to the field that I call *illusio*. They may want to overturn the relations of force within the field, but, for that very reason, they grant recognition to the stakes, they are not indifferent. Wanting to undertake a revolution in a field is to accord the essential of what the field tacitly demands, namely that it is important, that the game played is sufficiently important for one to want to undertake a revolution in it.

Among people who occupy opposing positions in a field and who seem to be radically opposed in everything, there is a hidden, tacit accord about the fact that it is worth the effort to struggle for the things that are in play in the field. Primary apoliticism, which continues to grow because the political field increasingly tends to close in on itself and to function without referring to its clientele (that is, it is somewhat like the artistic field), rests on a sort of confused awareness of the profound complicity between the adversaries inserted in the same field: they disagree with one another, but they at least agree about the object of disagreement.

Libido would also be entirely pertinent for saying what I have called *illusio*, or investment. Each field imposes a tacit entrance fee: "Let no one enter here who is not a geometrician," that is, no one should enter who is not ready to die for a theorem. If I had to summarize in an image all that I have just said about the notion of field, and about *illusio* which is at the same time the condition and the product of the field's functioning, I would recall a sculpture found at the Auch cathedral, in the Gers, which represents two monks struggling over the prior's staff. In a world which, like the religious universe, and above all the monastic universe, is the site par excellence of *Ausserweltlich*, of the extraworldly of disinterestendness in the naive sense of the term, one finds people who struggle over a staff, whose value exists only for those who are in the game, caught up in the game.

One of the tasks of sociology is to determine how the social world constitutes the biological libido, an undifferentiated impulse, as a specific social libido. There are in effect as many kinds of libido as there are fields: the work of socialization of the libido is precisely what transforms impulses into specific interests, socially constituted interests which only exist in relation to a social space in which certain things are important and others don't matter and for socialized agents who are constituted in such a way as to make distinctions corresponding to the objective differences in that space.

Against Utilitarianism

What is experienced as obvious in *illusio* appears as an illusion to those who do not participate in the obviousness because they do not participate in the game. Knowledge seeks to defuse this sort of hold that social games have on socialized agents. This is not easy to do: one does not free oneself through a simple conversion of consciousness. Agents well-adjusted to the game are possessed by the game and doubtless all the more so the better they master it. For example, one of the privileges associated with the fact of being born in a game is that one can avoid cynicism since one has a feel for the game; like a good tennis player, one positions oneself not where the ball is but where it will be; one invests oneself and one invests not where the profit is, but where it will be. Reconversions, through which one moves toward new genres, new disciplines, new subjects, etc., are experienced as *conversions*.

How do some go about reducing this description of the practical relationship between agents and fields to a utilitarianist vision (and *illusio* to the interest of utilitarianism)? First, they pretend agents are moved by conscious reasons, as if they consciously posed the objectives of their action and acted in such a way as to obtain the maximum efficacy with the least cost. The second, anthropological hypothesis: they reduce everything that can motivate agents to economic interest, to monetary profit. They assume, in a word, that the principle of action is well-thought-out economic interest and its objective is material profit, posed consciously through rational calculation. I want to attempt to show how all of my work has consisted in rejecting these two reductions.

To the reduction of conscious calculation, I oppose the relationship of ontological complicity between thc habitus and the field. Between agents and the social world there is a relationship of infraconscious, infralinguistic complicity: in their practice agents constantly engage in theses which are not posed as such. Does a human behavior really always have as an end, that is, as a goal, the result which is the end, in the sense of conclusion, or term, of that behavior? I think not. What is, therefore, this very strange relationship to the social or natural world in which agents aim at certain ends without posing them as such? Social agents who have a feel for the game, who have embodied a host of practical schemes of perception and appreciation functioning as instruments of reality construction, as principles of vision and division of the universe in which they act, do not need to pose the objectives of their practice as ends. They are not like *subjects* faced with an object (or, even less, a problem) that will be constituted as such by an intellectual act of cognition; they are, as it is said, absorbed in their affairs (one could also say their "doing"): they are present at the coming moment, the doing, the deed (*pragma*, in Greek), the immediate correlate of practice (*praxis*) which is not posed as an object of thought, as a possible aimed for in a project, but which is inscribed in the present of the game.

Ordinary analyses of temporal experience confuse two relationships to the future or the past which Husserl clearly distinguishes with *Ideen*: the relationship to the future that might be called a *project*, and which poses the future as future, that is, as a possible constituted as such, thus as possibly happening or not, is opposed to the relationship to the future that he calls *protension* or pre-perceptive anticipation, a relationship to a future that is not a future, to a future that is almost present. Although I do not see the hidden sides of a cube, they are quasi present, they are "presented" in a relationship of belief which is that which we accord to something we perceive. They are not aimed for in a project, as equally possible or impossible; they are there, with the doxic modality of that which is directly perceived.

In fact, these pre-perceptive anticipations, a sort of practical induction based on previous experience, are not given to a pure subject, a universal transcendental consciousness. They are the fact of the habitus as a feel for the game. Having the feel for the game is having the game under the skin; it is to master in a practical way the future of the game; it is to have a sense of the history of the game. While the bad player is always off tempo, always too early or too late, the good player is the one who *anticipates*, who is ahead of the game. Why can she get ahead of the flow of the game? Because she has the immanent tendencies of the game in her body, in an incorporated state: she embodies the game.

The habitus fulfills a function which another philosophy consigns to a transcendental conscience: it is a socialized body, a structured body, a body which has incorporated the immanent structures of a world or of a particular sector of that world – a field – and which structures the perception of that world as well as action in that world. For example, the opposition between theory and practice is found both in the objective structure of disciplines (mathematics is opposed to geology as philosophy is opposed to geography) and in the mind of professors who, in their judgments of students, bring into play practical schemes, often associated with couples of adjectives, which are the embodied equivalent of those objective structures. And when the embodied structures and the objective structures are in agreement, when perception is constructed according to the structures of what is perceived, everything seems obvious and goes without saying. It is the doxical experience in which one attributes to the world a deeper belief than all beliefs (in the ordinary sense), since it does not think of itself as a belief.

Against the intellectualist tradition of the *cogito*, of knowledge as a relation between a subject and an object, etc., in order to account for human behaviors it is necessary to admit that they rest constantly on non-thetic theses; that they posit futures that are not aimed for as futures. The paradox of the human sciences is that they must constantly distrust the philosophy of action inherent in models such as game theory, which are apparently used to understand social universes resembling games. It is true that most human behaviors take place within playing fields; thus, they do not have as a principle a strategic intention such as that postulated by game theory. In other words, social agents have "strategies" which only rarely have a true strategic intention as a principle.

This is another way of expressing the opposition that Husserl establishes between protension and project, the opposition between the *preoccupation* (which could be used to translate Heidegger's *Fürsorge*, removing its undesirable connotations) and the *plan* as a design for the future in which the subject thinks of herself as positing a future and mobilizing all disposable means by reference to that future posited as such, as an end before explicitly being attained. The player's preoccupation or anticipation is immediately present in something that is not immediately perceived and immediately available, but it is as if it were already there. The player who hits a ball to the opposite court acts in the present in relation to a coming moment (I say coming moment rather than future) which is quasi present, which is inscribed in the very physiognomy of the present, of the adversary running toward the right. She does not pose this future in a project (I can go to the right or not): she hits the ball to the left because her adversary is going to the right, because he is already, as it were, to the right. She makes up her mind in function of a quasi present inscribed in the present.

Practice has a logic which is not that of logic, and thus to apply practical logic to logical logic is to run the risk of destroying the logic one wants to describe with the instrument used to describe it. These problems, that I posed 20 years ago, in *Outline of a Theory of Practice*,[1] are brought to light today with the construction of expert systems and artificial intelligence: one sees that in practice social agents (whether a doctor who makes a diagnosis or a professor who grades an examination) possess extremely complex classificatory systems which are never constituted as such and which can only be so constituted at the cost of a considerable amount of work.

To substitute a practical relationship of pre-occupation, immediate presence to a coming moment inscribed in the present, with a rational, calculating consciousness, positing ends as such, as possibles, is to raise the question of cynicism, which poses unmentionable ends as such. If my analysis is correct, one can, for example, be adjusted to the necessities of a game – one can have a magnificent academic career – without ever needing to give oneself such an objective. Very often researchers, because they are inspired by a will to demystify, tend to act as if agents always had as an end, in the sense of goal, the end, in the sense of conclusion, of their trajectory. Transforming the journey into a project, they act as if the consecrated university professor, whose career they study, had in mind the ambition of becoming a professor at the Collège de France from the moment when he chose a discipline, a thesis director, a topic of research. They give a more or less cynical calculating consciousness as the principle of agents' behaviors in a field (the two monks who clash over the prior's staff, or two professors who struggle to impose their theory of action).

If what I am saying is true, it happens quite differently. Agents who clash over the ends under consideration can be possessed by those ends. They may be ready to die for those ends, independently of all considerations of specific, lucrative profits, career profits, or other forms of profit. Their relation to the end involved is not at all the conscious calculation of usefulness that utilitarianism lends them, a philosophy that is readily applied to the actions of others. They have a feel for the game; for example, in games where it is necessary to be "disinterested" in order to succeed, they can undertake, in a spontaneously disinterested manner, actions in accordance with their interests. There are quite paradoxical situations that a philosophy of consciousness precludes us from understanding.

I now come to the second reduction, which consists of reducing everything to lucrative interest, to reduce the ends of the action to economic ends. The refutation of this point is relatively easier. In effect, the principle of error lies in what is traditionally called economism, that is, considering the laws of functioning of one social field among others, namely the economic field, as being valid for all fields. At the very foundation of the theory of fields is the observation (which is already found in Spencer, Durkheim, Weber . . .) that the social world is the site of a process of progressive differentiation. Thus, Durkheim endlessly recalled, one observes that initially, in archaic societies and even in numerous precapitalist societies, social universes which in our society are differentiated (such as religion, art, science) are still undifferentiated; one thus observes in them a polysemy and a multifunctionality (a word that Durkheim often employs in *The Elementary Forms of Religious Life*) of human behaviors, which can be interpreted at the same time as religious, economic, aesthetic, and so forth.

The evolution of societies tends to make universes (which I call fields) emerge which are autonomous and have their own laws. Their fundamental laws are often tautologies. That of the economic field, which has been elaborated by utilitarian philosophers: business is business; that of the artistic field, which has been posed explicitly by the so-called art for art's sake school: the end of art is art, art has no other end than art . . . Thus, we have social universes which have a fundamental law, a *nomos* which is independent from the laws of other universes, which are *auto-nomes*, which evaluate what is done in them, the stakes at play, according to principles and criteria that are irreducible to those of other

universes. We are thus light years from economism, which consists of applying to all universes the *nomos* characteristic of the
economic field. This amounts to forgetting that the economic
field itself was constructed through a process of differentiation,
by positing that the economic is not reducible to the laws which
govern the domestic economy, to *philia*, as Aristotle would say,
and vice versa.

This process of differentiation or autonomization thus leads
to the constitution of universes which have different, irreducible
"fundamental laws" (an expression borrowed from Kelsen), and
which are the site of particular forms of interest. What makes
people enter and compete in the scientific field is not the same thing
that makes them enter and compete in the economic field. The
most striking example is that of the artistic field which is constituted in the nineteenth century by taking the reverse of economic
law as its fundamental law. The process which begins with the
Renaissance and reaches its full realization in the second half
of the nineteenth century, with what is called art for art's sake,
amounts to completely dissociating lucrative ends and the specific objectives of the universe – with, for example, the opposition
between commercial art and pure art. Pure art, the only true form
of art according to the specific norms of the autonomous field,
rejects commercial ends, that is, the subordination of the artist,
and above all his or her production, to external demands and to
the sanctions of those demands, which are economic sanctions.
It is constituted on the basis of a fundamental law which is the
negation (or disavowal) of the economy: let no one enter here if
he or she has commercial concerns.

Another field that is constituted on a base of the same type of
disavowal of interest is the bureaucratic field. The Hegelian philosophy of state, a sort of ideal bureaucratic self, is the representation
that the bureaucratic field seeks to give itself and give of itself,
that is, the image of a universe whose fundamental law is public
service; a universe in which social agents have no personal interest and sacrifice their own interests to the public, to public service,
to the universal.

The theory of the process of differentiation and autonomization
of social universes having different fundamental laws leads to a
breaking up of the notion of interest; there are as many forms of
libido, as many kinds of "interest," as there are fields. Every field,

in producing itself, produces a form of interest which, from the point of view of another field, may seem like disinterestedness (or absurdity, lack of realism, folly, etc.). One thus sees the difficulty in applying the principle of the theory of sociological knowledge that I announced at the outset and that argues that there is nothing without reason. Is a sociology of these universes whose fundamental law is disinterestedness (in the sense of a refusal of economic interest) still possible? For it to be possible, there must exist a form of interest that one can describe, for the sake of communication, and at the risk of falling into a reductionist vision, as interest in disinterestedness or, better still, as a disinterested or generous *disposition*.

Here it is necessary to bring in everything that touches on the symbolic: symbolic capital, symbolic interest, symbolic profit . . . I call symbolic capital any kind of capital (economic, cultural, academic, or social) when it is perceived according to the categories of perception, the principles of vision and division, the systems of classification, the classificatory schemes, the cognitive schemata, which are, at least in part, the product of the embodiment of the objective structures of the field in consideration, that is, of the structure of the distribution of capital in the field being considered. Symbolic capital which makes one bow before Louis XIV – that makes one court him, that allows him to give orders and have his orders obeyed, that permits him to demean, demote, or consecrate, etc. – only exists inasmuch as all the small differences, the subtle marks of distinction in etiquette and rank, in practices and in dress, which make up the life of the court, are perceived by people who know and recognize practically (they have embodied it) a principle of differentiation that permits them to recognize all these differences and to give them value, who are ready, in a word, to die over a quarrel of hats. Symbolic capital is capital with a cognitive base, which rests on cognition and recognition.

Disinterestedness as Passion

Having very summarily evoked the basic concepts which I see as indispensable for thinking about reasonable action – habitus, field, interest or *illusio*, symbolic capital – I again turn to the problem of disinterestedness. Are disinterested behaviors possible, and, if so, how and under what conditions? If one stays within a philosophy of consciousness, it is obvious that one can only respond to the question negatively and that all apparently disinterested actions conceal intentions to maximize a certain kind of profit. In introducing the notion of symbolic capital (and symbolic profit), we in some way radicalize the questioning of the naive vision: the most holy actions – asceticism or the most extreme devotion – may always be suspect (historically they have been, through certain extreme forms of rigorism) of being inspired by the search for the symbolic profit of saintliness, or celebrity, etc.[2] At the beginning of *The Court Society*, Norbert Elias cites the example of a duke who gives a purse full of crowns to his son. When he questions him six months later and the son boasts of not having spent the money, the duke takes the purse and throws it out the window. He thus gives his son a lesson of disinterestedness, gratuitousness, and nobility; but it is also a lesson of investment, of the investment of symbolic capital, which suits an aristocratic universe. (The same would hold for a Kabyle man of honor.)

In fact, there exist social universes in which the search for strictly economic profit can be discouraged by explicit norms or tacit injunctions. "Noblesse oblige" means that it is that *noblesse* or nobility that impedes the nobleman from doing certain things and allows him to do others. Because it forms part of his definition, of his superior essence, to be disinterested, generous, he cannot be otherwise, "it is stronger than him." On the one hand, the social universe requires him to be generous; on the other, he is disposed to be generous through brutal lessons such as that related by Elias, but also by innumerable, often tacit and quasi-imperceptible, lessons of daily existence, such as insinuations, reproaches, silences, avoidances. The behaviors of honor in aristocratic or precapitalist societies have at their origin an economy of symbolic goods based on the collective repression of interest and, more broadly, the truth of production and circulation, which tends to produce "disinterested" habitus, anti-economic habitus, disposed to repress interests, in the narrow sense of the term (that is, the pursuit of economic profits), especially in domestic relations.

Why is it important to think in terms of habitus? Why is it important to think of the field as a space which one has not produced and in which one is born, and not an arbitrarily instituted game? Because it permits us to understand that there are disinter-

ested forms of behavior which do not have as a principle the calculation of disinterestedness, the calculated intention to surmount
calculation or to show that one is capable of surmounting it.
This goes against La Rochefoucauld, who, being the product of a
society of honor, understood quite well the economy of symbolic
goods, but who, because the Jansenist worm had already slipped
into the aristocratic apple, begins to say that aristocratic attitudes
are in fact the supreme forms of calculation, calculation of the
second degree (this is the example of Augustus's clemency). In
a well-constituted society of honor, La Rochefoucauld's analyses
are incorrect; they apply to societies of honor which are already
in crisis, like those I studied in *Le Déracinement*,[3] and where the
values of honor crumble as monetary exchanges, and through them
the spirit of calculation, are generalized; this process goes hand in
hand with the objective possibility of calculating (the work and
value of a man begin to be evaluated in monetary terms, which
is unthinkable). In well-constituted societies of honor, there may
be disinterested habitus, and the habitus–field relationship is such
that, in the form of spontaneity or *passion*, in the mode of "it is
stronger than me," disinterested acts can be carried out. To a certain extent, the aristocrat cannot do otherwise than be generous,
through loyalty to his group and to himself as a person worthy of
being a member of the group. That is what "noblesse oblige"
means. Nobility is nobility as a corporate body, as a group which,
incorporated, embodied as disposition, habitus, becomes the subject of noble practices, and obliges the noble to act in a noble
fashion.

When official representations of what man officially is in a considered social space become habitus, they become the real principle of practices. Without doubt the social universes within which
disinterestedness is the official norm are not necessarily governed
throughout by disinterestedness: behind the appearance of piety,
virtue, disinterestedness, there are subtle, camouflaged interests; the
bureaucrat is not just the servant of the state, he is also the one
who puts the state at his service . . . Thus, an agent does not live
with impunity under the permanent invocation of virtue, because
he is caught up in mechanisms, and there are sanctions which
remind him of the obligation of disinterestedness.

Consequently, the question of the possibility of virtue can be
brought back to the question of the social conditions of possibility

of the universes in which the durable dispositions for disinterestedness may be constituted and, once constituted, may find objective conditions for constant reinforcement and become the principle of a permanent practice of virtue. Within such universes, in the same sense, virtuous actions regularly exist with a decent statistical frequency and not in the form of the heroism of a few virtuous people. Durable virtues cannot be established on a pure decision of conscience, that is, in the Sartrean sense, on something like an oath.

If disinterestedness is sociologically possible, it can be so only through the encounter between habitus predisposed to disinterestedness and the universes in which disinterestedness is rewarded. Among these universes, the most typical are, along with the family and the whole economy of domestic exchanges, the different fields of cultural production, the literary field, the artistic field, the scientific field, and so forth, microcosms which are constituted on the basis of an inversion of the fundamental law of the economic world and in which the law of economic interest is suspended. This does not mean that they do not know other forms of interest: the sociology of art or literature unveils (or unmasks) and analyzes the specific interests which are constituted by the field's functioning (which led Breton to break the arm of a rival in a poetic dispute), and for which one is ready to die.

The Profits of Universalization

I must still ask a question that I hesitate to raise: how does it happen that it can be almost universally observed that there are profits in submitting to the universal? I believe that a comparative anthropology would permit us to say that there is a universal recognition of the recognition of the universal; it is a universal of social practices recognizing as valuable forms of behavior that have submission, even visible submission, to the universal as a principle. Let me give an example. Working on matrimonial exchange in Algeria, I observed that there was an official norm (one should marry the parallel cousin) and that this norm was actually little observed in practice: the rate of marriage with the patrilineal parallel cousin is on the order of 3 percent, and around 6 percent in marabout families, which are more rigid. That being said, since this norm remains the official truth of practices, certain agents, knowing how to play the game and impelled by the need to "hide their shame" or some other constraint, were able, in the logic of pious hypocrisy, to transfigure the duty of a marriage with the parallel cousin into a choice: by "getting into line" with the official norm, they managed to add profits provided by conformity with the universal to profits that an "interested" strategy provides.

If it is true that every society offers the possibility of a profit of the universal, behaviors with a universal pretension will be universally exposed to suspicion. This is the anthropological basis of the Marxist critique of ideology as the universalization of a particular interest: the ideologue is the one who posits as universal, as disinterested, that which is in accordance with their particular interest. The fact that there are profits of the universal and of universalization, the fact that one obtains such profits in rendering homage, albeit hypocritically, to the universal, in dressing in the universal a behavior in fact determined by particular interest (a man marries the parallel cousin because he did not find another, but he leads others to believe that he did so out of respect for the law), the fact therefore that there can be profits of virtue and reason is without doubt one of the great motors of virtue and reason in history. Without bringing in any metaphysical hypothesis (even disguised as an empirical statement, as in Habermas), one can say that reason has a basis in history and that if reason progresses even the slightest, it is because there are interests in universalization and because, universally, but above all in certain universes, such as the artistic or scientific field, it is better to seem disinterested rather than interested, as generous and altruistic rather than egotistical. And strategies of universalization, which are at the origin of all official *norms* and *forms* (with everything they may have of a mystifying nature) and which rest on the universal existence of profits of universalization, are what make the universal universally possess not inconsiderable chances of succeeding.

Thus, for the question of knowing if virtue is possible, one can substitute the question of knowing if one can create universes in which people have an interest in the universal. Machiavelli says that the republic is a universe in which citizens have an interest in virtue. The genesis of a universe of this sort is not conceivable if one does not posit the motor, which is the universal recognition of the universal, that is, the official recognition of the primacy of the group and its interests over the individual and the individual's interests, which all groups profess in the very fact of affirming themselves as groups.

The critique of suspicion reminds us that all universal values are in fact particular, universalized values, which are thus subject to suspicion (universal culture is the culture of the dominants, etc.). A first, inevitable moment of the recognition of the social world, this critique should not make us forget that all the things the dominants celebrate, and in which they celebrate themselves by so celebrating (culture, disinterestedness, the pure, Kantian morality, Kantian aesthetics, etc., everything which I objectified, perhaps somewhat crudely, at the end of *Distinction*), can only fulfill their symbolic function of legitimation precisely because they benefit in principle from universal recognition – people cannot openly deny them without denying their own humanity; but, for this reason, the behaviors that render them homage, sincere or not, it matters little, are assured a form of symbolic profit (notably of conformity and distinction) which, even if it is not sought as such, suffices to ground them in sociological reason and, in giving them a *raison d'être*, assure them a reasonable probability of existing.

I return, in conclusion, to the bureaucracy, one of these universes which, using the law, assumes submission to the universal, to the general interest, to public service, as law, and which recognizes itself in the philosophy of the bureaucracy as a universal class, neutral, above conflicts, at the service of public interest, of rationality (or of rationalization). The social groups which constructed the Prussian bureaucracy or the French bureaucracy had an interest in the universal, and they had to invent the universal (the law, the idea of public service, the idea of general interest, etc.) and, if one may put it this way, domination in the name of the universal in order to accede to domination.

One of the difficulties of the political struggle today is that the dominants, technocrats or epistemocrats on the right or the left, are hand in glove with reason and the universal: one makes one's way through universes in which more and more technical, rational justifications will be necessary in order to dominate and in which the dominated can and must also use reason to defend themselves against domination, because the dominants must increasingly invoke reason, and science, to exert their domination. This makes the progress of reason without doubt go hand in hand with the development of highly rationalized forms of domination (as one sees, today, with the use that is made of a technique like the survey); it also creates a situation in which sociology, alone in a position to bring these mechanisms to light, must choose now more than ever between putting its rational instruments of knowledge at the service of an increasingly rational domination, or rationally analyzing domination and especially the contribution that rational knowledge can make to domination.

Notes

1 Pierre Bourdieu, *Outline of a Theory of Practice*, trans. Richard Nice (Cambridge: Cambridge University Press, 1977).
2 See, on this point, Gilbert Dagron's article, "L'homme sans honneur ou le saint scandaleux," *Annales ESC* (July–Aug. 1990), pp. 929–39.
3 Pierre Bourdieu and Abdelmalek Sayad, *Le Déracinement. La crise de l'agriculture traditionelle en Algérie* (Paris: Éditions de Minuit, 1964).

5

The Economy of Symbolic Goods

T he question I am going to examine is one that I have not ceased asking from my first ethnological works on the Kabyle to my more recent research on the world of art and, more precisely, on the functioning of artistic patronage in modern societies. I would like to show that with the same instruments, one can analyze phenomena as different as exchanges of honor in a precapitalist society, or, in societies like our own, the action of foundations such as the Ford Foundation or the Fondation de France, exchanges between generations within a family, transactions in markets of cultural or religious goods, and so forth.

For obvious reasons, symbolic goods are spontaneously located by ordinary dichotomies (material/spiritual, body/spirit, etc.) on the side of the spiritual, and are thus often considered beyond the grasp of scientific analysis. For this reason, they represent a challenge I wanted to take up based on extremely different works: first, analyses I undertook of the functioning of the Kabyle economy, a perfect example of a precapitalist economy based on the negation of the economic in the sense we understand it; second, the research I carried out, at different moments and in different places (Kabylia, Béarn, etc.), on the functioning of the domestic economy, that is, on exchanges, within the family, between members of the household and between generations; third, analyses of what I call the economy of the offering, that is, the type of transaction that occurs between churches and their followers; and, finally, studies of the economy of cultural goods, with the research I have done on the literary field and on the bureaucratic economy. Based on the knowledge acquired through the analysis of these phenomenally very different social universes, which have never been brought together as such, I would like to try to extract the general principles of an economy of symbolic goods.

In one of my very first books I wrote, with the daring associated with the arrogance (and ignorance) of youth (but perhaps it is because I dared then that I can do what I do today . . .), that sociology's role was the construction of a general theory of the economy of practices. What certain adepts of *fast-reading* (including many professors, unfortunately) saw as an expression of economism, marked, to the contrary, a desire to wrest from economism (Marxist or neomarginalist) precapitalist economies and entire sectors of so-called capitalist economies which do not function according to the law of interest seen as the search for the maximization of (monetary) profit. The economic universe is made up of several economic worlds, endowed with specific "rationalities," at the same time assuming and demanding "reasonable" (more than rational) dispositions adjusted to the regularities inscribed in each of them, to the "practical reason" which characterizes them. The worlds I am going to describe have in common the fact that they create the objective conditions for social agents to have an interest in "disinterestedness," which seems paradoxical.

Retrospectively, I realized that in my understanding of the Kabyle economy I used, more unconsciously than consciously, the practical experience that I, like everyone (we all issue from family universes), had of the domestic economy and that often contradicts our experience of the economy of calculation. But inversely, having understood this noneconomic economy, I was able to return to the domestic economy or the economy of offerings with a system of questions I believe I would not have been able to construct if I had dedicated my life to the sociology of the family.

Gifts and Equivalent Exchanges

Very briefly, since I cannot assume knowledge of what I wrote in *The Logic of Practice*, in a return to certain analyses of that book I will to try to clarify certain general principles of the symbolic economy, beginning with the essential elements of the analysis of gift exchange. Mauss described the exchange of gifts as a discontinuous succession of generous acts; Lévi-Strauss defined it as a structure of transcendent reciprocity of acts of exchange, where the gift results in a countergift. In my case, I indicated that what was absent from these two analyses was the determinant role of the temporal interval between the gift and the countergift, the fact that in practically all societies, it is tacitly admitted that one does not immediately reciprocate for a gift received, since it would amount to a refusal. I asked myself about the function of that interval: why must the countergift be deferred and different? And I showed that the interval had the function of creating a screen between the gift and the countergift and allowing two perfectly symmetrical acts to appear as unique and unrelated acts. If I can experience my gift as a gratuitous, generous gift, which is not to be paid back, it is first because there is a risk, no matter how small, that there will not be a return (there are always ungrateful people), therefore a suspense, an uncertainty, which makes the interval between the moment of giving and the moment of receiving exist as such. In societies like Kabyle society, the constraint is in fact very great and the freedom not to return the gift is infinitesimal. But the possibility exists and, for the same reason, certainty is not absolute. Everything occurs as if the time interval, which distinguishes the exchange of gifts from swapping, existed to permit the giver to experience the gift as a gift without reciprocity, and the one who gives a countergift to experience it as gratuitous and not determined by the initial gift.

In reality, the structural truth that Lévi-Strauss brought to light is not unknown. In Kabylia I collected numerous proverbs which say roughly that a present is a misfortune because, in the final analysis, it must be reciprocated. (The same occurs with words or challenges.) In any case, the initial act is an attack on the freedom of the one who receives it. It is threatening: it obligates one to reciprocate, and to reciprocate beyond the original gift; furthermore, it creates obligations, it is a way to possess, by creating people obliged to reciprocate.[1]

But this structural truth is collectively repressed. The time interval can only be understood by hypothesizing that the giver and the receiver collaborate, without knowing it, in a work of dissimulation tending to deny the truth of the exchange, the exchange of exact equivalents, which represents the destruction of the exchange of gifts. Here we touch on a very difficult problem: sociology, if it limits itself to an objectivist description, reduces the exchange of gifts to swapping and can no longer establish the difference between an exchange of gifts and an act of credit. Thus, what is important in gift exchange is the fact that through the interposed time interval, those involved in the exchange work, without knowing or planning, to mask or repress the objective truth of their action, a truth which the sociologist unveils, but at the risk of describing as cynical calculation an act which claims to be disinterested and which must be taken as such, in its lived truth, which the theoretical model must also consider and explain.

We thus have an initial property of the economy of symbolic exchanges: practices always have double truths, which are difficult to hold together. Analysis must take note of this duality. In a more general sense, we can only understand the economy of symbolic goods if, from the outset, we accept taking this ambiguity seriously, an ambiguity which is not made by the scientist, but which is present in reality itself, a sort of contradiction between subjective truth and objective reality (which sociology approaches through statistics, ethnology through structural analysis). This duality is rendered possible, and viable, through a sort of *self-deception* or self-mystification. But this individual *self-deception* is sustained by a collective *self-deception*, a veritable *collective misrecognition*[2] inscribed in objective structures (the logic of honor which governs all exchanges – of words, of women, of murders, etc.) and in mental structures,[3] excluding the possibility of thinking or acting otherwise.

If agents can be at the same time mystifiers, of themselves and others, and mystified, it is because they have been immersed from childhood in a universe where gift exchange is socially *instituted* in dispositions and beliefs. Such exchange thus shares none of the paradoxes that are made to emerge artificially when, like Jacques Derrida in the recent book *Passions*, one relies on the logic of consciousness and the free choice of an isolated individual. When one forgets that the giver and the receiver are prepared and inclined through the whole work of socialization to enter, without intention or calculation of profit, generous exchange, whose logic is objectively imposed on them, one may conclude that the gratuitous gift does not exist, or is impossible, since two agents can only be conceived as calculators giving of themselves because of a subjective plan to do what they do objectively, according to the Lévi-Straussian model, that is, an exchange obeying the logic of reciprocity.

And here we find another property of the economy of symbolic exchanges: the *taboo of making things explicit* (whose form par excellence is the price). To say what it really is, to declare the truth of the exchange, or, as is often said, "the truth of the price" (before giving a present, we remove the price tag . . .), is to destroy the exchange. We see in passing that forms of behavior such as the exchange of gifts pose a difficult problem for sociology, which, by definition, makes things explicit: it is obligated to state that which goes without saying and which should remain tacit and unsaid at the risk of being destroyed as such.

We can verify these analyses and confirm the taboo of making things explicit that the economy of symbolic exchanges conceals in a description of the effects produced by setting a price. Just as one can use the economy of symbolic exchanges as an analyzer of the economy of economic exchange, one can, inversely, ask the economy of economic exchange to serve as an analyzer of the economy of symbolic exchanges. Thus, the *price*, which characterizes the economy of economic exchanges in opposition to the economy of symbolic exchanges, functions as a symbolic expression of consensus regarding the exchange rate implied in every economic exchange. This consensus regarding the exchange rate is also present in an economy of symbolic exchanges, but its terms and conditions are left implicit. In the exchange of gifts, the price should be left implicit (this is the example of the price tag): I do not want to know the truth of the price, and I do not want the other person to know it either. Everything occurs as if there were an agreement to avoid explicitly reaching an agreement about the relative value of the things exchanged, by refusing all prior explicit definitions of the terms of exchange, that is, of the price (which translates, as Viviana Zelizer has remarked, as a taboo on the use of money in certain exchanges – one does not give a salary to one's son or spouse, and the young Kabyle who asks his father for a salary causes a scandal).

The language I use has finalist connotations and may lead one to think that people deliberately close their eyes to this reality; in fact, it is necessary to say "everything occurs as if." To refuse the logic of the price is a way to refuse calculation and calculability. The fact that the consensus regarding the exchange rate is explicit is what renders calculability and predictability possible: one knows what to expect. But it is also what ruins every economy of symbolic exchanges, an economy of things without price, in the double sense of the term. (To speak of the price of priceless things,[4] as one is often forced to do because of the needs of the analysis, is to introduce a contradiction in terms.)

Silence about the truth of the exchange is a shared silence. Economists who can only conceive of rational, calculated action in the name of a finalist and intellectualist philosophy of action speak of *common knowledge*: information is common knowledge when one can say that everyone knows that everyone knows that everyone possesses certain information or, as is often said, when it is an open secret. We might be tempted to say that the objective truth of the exchange of gifts is, in a sense, common knowledge: I know that you know that, when I give you a gift, I know that you will reciprocate, etc. But making the open secret explicit is taboo. It must remain implicit. There are myriad objective social mechanisms embodied in each agent which make the very idea of divulging that secret sociologically unthinkable (saying, for example: "let's stop pretending that reciprocal exchanges are generous gifts, that's hypocritical," and so forth).

But to speak, as I have done, of common knowledge (or of *self-deception*) is to remain within a philosophy of consciousness and act as if each agent were inhabited by a double consciousness, a split consciousness, divided against itself, *consciously* repressing a truth which it otherwise knows (I am not inventing anything: suffice to read Jon Elster, *Ulysses and the Sirens*). One can only account for all double behaviors, without duplicity, of the economy of symbolic exchanges by abandoning the theory of action as a product of an intentional consciousness, an explicit project, an explicit intention oriented toward an explicitly stated goal (especially that which clarifies the objective analysis of exchange).

The theory of action that I propose (with the notion of habitus) amounts to saying that most human actions have as a basis something quite different from intention, that is, acquired dispositions which make it so that an action can and should be interpreted as oriented toward one objective or another without anyone being able to claim that that objective was a conscious design (it is here that the "everything occurs as if" is very important). The best example of such a disposition is without doubt the feel for the game: the player, having deeply internalized the regularities of a game, does what he must do at the moment it is necessary, without needing to ask explicitly what is to be done. He does not need to know consciously what he does in order to do it and even less to raise explicitly the question (except in some critical situations) of knowing explicitly what others might do in return, as the view of chess or bridge players that certain economists (above all those who use game theory) attribute to agents would let us believe.

Thus, the exchange of gifts (or women, or services, etc.), conceived as a paradigm of the economy of symbolic goods, is opposed to the equivalent exchanges of the economic economy as long as its basis is not a calculating subject, but rather an agent socially disposed to enter, without intention or calculation, into the game of exchange. It is for this reason that he ignores or denies its objective truth as an economic exchange. We can see another confirmation of this in the fact that, in this economy, either one leaves economic interest implicit, or, if one states it, it is through euphemisms, that is, in a language of denial. Euphemisms permit the naming of the unnameable, that is, in an economy of symbolic goods, the economic, in the ordinary sense of the term, the exchange of exact equivalents.

I said "euphemism," I could have said "imposition of form." Symbolic work consists both of imposing forms and observing formalities. The group requires that formalities be observed, that one honor the humanity of others by asserting one's own humanity, by affirming one's "point of spiritualist honor." There is no society that does not render homage to those who render homage to it in seeming to refuse the law of selfish interest. What is required is not that one do absolutely everything that one should, but rather that one at least give indications of trying to do so. Social agents are not expected to be perfectly in order, but rather to observe order, to give visible signs that, if they can, they will respect the rules (that is how I understand the formula: "hypocrisy is a homage that vice renders to virtue"). Practical euphemisms are a kind of homage rendered to the social order and to the values the social order exalts, all the while knowing that they are doomed to be violated.

Symbolic Alchemy

This structural hypocrisy is imposed particularly on the dominants, according to the formula of "noblesse oblige." For the Kabyle, the economic economy as we practice it is a women's economy.[5] Men are held to a point of honor, which prohibits all concessions to the logic of the economic economy. The honorable man cannot say: "You will repay me before the beginning of plowing"; he leaves the date of payment vague. Or: "You will give me four hundredweights of wheat and, in exchange, I will lend you an ox." Women, on the other hand, tell the truth about prices and dates of payment; they can allow themselves to tell the economic truth since they are excluded from the economy of symbolic exchanges (at least as subjects). And this is still true in our societies. In the issue of the journal *Actes de la Recherche* entitled "L'Économie da la maison" ("The Domestic Economy"), for example, one can see that men often manage by making women do what they themselves cannot do without demeaning themselves, such as asking the price.[6]

The denial of the economy is accomplished through a work objectively oriented toward the transfiguration of economic relations, and in particular of relations of exploitation (man/woman, elder brother/younger brother, master/servant), a transfiguration through language (with euphemisms) but also through acts. There are practical euphemisms. The exchange of gifts is one such euphemism thanks to the time interval (one does what one does, while seeming not to do it). The agents engaged in an economy of symbolic exchanges expend a considerable part of their energy elaborating these euphemisms. (This is one of the reasons why the economic economy is much more economic. For example, when, instead of giving a "personal" present, that is, a present adjusted to the presumed taste of the receiver, one gives, through laziness or convenience, a check, one economizes the work of looking, which assumes the attention and care necessary for the present to be adapted to the person, to his or her tastes, to arrive at the right time, etc., and also that its "value" is not directly reducible to its monetary value.) The economic economy is more economic, therefore, to the extent that it permits one to save the work of symbolic construction objectively tending to conceal the objective truth of practice.

The most interesting example of this sort of symbolic alchemy is the transfiguration of relations of domination and exploitation. Gift exchange can be established between equals and contribute to reinforcing "communion" or solidarity through communication, which creates social ties. But it can also be established between agents who are actually or potentially unequal, such as in the potlatch which, if we are to believe those who have described it, institutes durable relations of symbolic domination, relations of domination based on communication, knowledge and recognition (in the double sense of the term). Among the Kabyle, women exchange little presents continuously, on a daily basis, which weave social relations on which rest many important things concerning, notably, the reproduction of the group, while men are responsible for large, discontinuous, extra-ordinary exchanges.

From ordinary acts to extraordinary acts of exchange, of which the potlatch is the extreme example (as an act of giving beyond the possibilities of return, which puts the receiver in an obliged and dominated state), the difference is only of degree. In even the most equal gift, the virtuality of the effect of domination exists. And the most unequal gift implies, despite everything, an act of exchange, a symbolic act of the recognition of equality in humanity which is only valid for those who possess categories of perception that allow them to perceive the exchange as exchange and to be interested by the object of exchange. A Trobiand islander only accepts coverings or shell necklaces suited to being recognized as gifts and causing his recognition if he is well socialized; otherwise, he has nothing to do with them, they do not interest him.

Symbolic acts always assume acts of knowledge and recognition, cognitive acts on the part of their recipients. For a symbolic exchange to function, the two parties must have identical categories of perception and appreciation. And this is also valid for acts of symbolic domination which, as seen clearly in the case of masculine domination,[7] are exerted with the objective complicity of the dominated, in that for a certain form of domination to be established, the dominated must apply to the acts of the dominant (and to all of their being) structures of perception which are the same as those the dominant use to produce those acts.

Symbolic domination (which is one way to define it) rests on misrecognition, and therefore on the recognition of the principles in whose name it is exerted. That is valid for masculine domination, but also for certain work relations, such as those which, in Arab countries, unite the *khammès* – a sort of sharecropper who receives a fifth of the harvest, or, according to Max Weber's description, an agricultural servant (in opposition to an agricultural worker) – to his master. Tenant farming for a fifth of the crop can only function, in societies which ignore constraints of the market or the state, if the sharecropper is in some way "domesticated," that is, *attached* by ties which are not those of law. And to become attached in this manner, the relation of domination and exploitation must be enchanted in such a way as to transform it into a domestic relationship of familiarity through a continuous series of acts capable of symbolically transfiguring it through euphemization (taking care of his son, marrying off his daughter, giving him presents, etc.).

In our societies, and at the very heart of the economic economy, we still find the logic of symbolic goods and the alchemy which transforms the truth of relations of domination, in paternalism. Another example would be the relationship between elder brothers and younger brothers as it exists in certain traditions ("the juniors of Gascogne"): in primogeniture societies, it is (we could say it was) necessary for the younger brother to submit – which often means, to renounce marriage and become, as indigenous cynicism says, a "servant without a salary" (or, as Galbraith said about the housewife, a "crypto-servant") – to love the elder's children as his own (everyone encourages him to do so), or to leave, join the army (the musketeers) or become a policeman or postal clerk.

The work of domestication (here, the "younger brother") that is necessary to transfigure the objective reality of a relation is the doing of the whole group, which encourages and rewards it. For the alchemy to function, as in the exchange of gifts, it must be sustained by the entire social structure, therefore by the mental structures and disposition produced by that social structure; there must be a market for like symbolic actions, there must be rewards, symbolic profits, often reconvertible into material profit, people must be able to have an interest in disinterestedness, a man who treats his servant well should be rewarded, with people saying of him: "He is an honest man, an honorable man!" But these relations remain very ambiguous and perverse. The *khammès* knows very well that he can manipulate his master: if he leaves claiming that his master treated him poorly and failed in his honor ("I who have done so much for him . . ."), dishonor again falls upon the master. And, likewise, the master can invoke the mistakes and shortcomings of the *khammès*, if they are known by everyone, to send him away, but if, exasperated because his *khammès* has stolen his olives, he loses his temper to the point of crushing him, of humiliating him beyond the limits, the situation turns in favor of the weak. These extremely complicated games, of an extraordinary refinement, unfold before the community tribunal, which also activates principles of perception and appreciation identical to those of the individuals concerned.

Recognition

One of the effects of symbolic violence is the transfiguration of relations of domination and submission into affective relations, the transformation of power into charisma or into the charm suited to evoke affective enchantment (for example, in relations between bosses and secretaries). The acknowledgment of debt becomes recognition, a durable *feeling* toward the author of the generous act, which can extend to affection or love, as can be seen particularly well in relations between generations.

Symbolic alchemy, such as I have described it, produces, to the benefit of the one who accomplishes acts of euphemization, transfiguration, or imposition of form, a capital of recognition which permits him to exert symbolic effects. This is what I call symbolic capital, thus conferring a rigorous meaning to what Max Weber designated with the term charisma, a purely descriptive concept, which he gives explicitly – at the beginning of the chapter on religion in *Economy and Society* – as an equivalent to what the Durkheimian school called *mana*. Symbolic capital is an ordinary property (physical strength, wealth, warlike valor, etc.) which, perceived by social agents endowed with the categories of perception and appreciation permitting them to perceive, know and recognize it, becomes symbolically efficient, like a veritable *magical power*: a property which, because it responds to socially constituted "collective expectations" and beliefs, exercises a sort of action from a distance, without physical contact. An order is given and obeyed: it is a quasi-magical act. But it is only an apparent exception to the law of the conservation of social energy. For the symbolic act to exert, without a visible expenditure of energy, this sort of magical efficacy, it is necessary for prior work – often invisible, and in any case forgotten or repressed – to have produced, among those who submit to the act of imposition or injunction, the dispositions necessary for them to feel they have obeyed without even posing the question of obedience. Symbolic violence is the violence which extorts submission, which is not perceived as such, based on "collective expectations" or socially inculcated beliefs. Like the theory of magic, the theory of symbolic violence rests on a theory of belief or, more precisely, on a theory of the production of belief, of the work of socialization necessary to produce agents endowed with the schemes of perception and appreciation that will permit them to perceive and obey the injunctions inscribed in a situation or discourse.

The belief I am describing is not an explicit belief, possessed explicitly as such in relation to a possibility of nonbelief, but rather an immediate adherence, a doxical submission to the injunctions of the world which is achieved when the mental structures of the one to whom the injunction is addressed are in accordance with the structures inscribed in the injunction addressed to him. In this case, one says that it went without saying, that there was nothing else to do. Faced with a challenge to his honor, he did what he had to do, what any true man of honor would do in a similar case, and he did it in a particularly accomplished manner (because there are degrees in the manner of obeying an injunction). Whoever responds to collective expectations, whoever, without having to calculate, is immediately adjusted to the exigencies inscribed in a situation, has all the profits of the market of symbolic goods. He has the profit of virtue, but also the profit of ease and elegance. He is all the more celebrated by the collective conscience given that he does, as if it went without saying, something that was, so to speak, the only thing to do, but something that it was possible for him not to do.

The last important characteristic is that symbolic capital is common to all members of a group. Since it is a being-perceived, which exists in the relations between properties held by agents and categories of perception (high/low, masculine/feminine, large/small, etc.) which constitute and construct social categories (those above/those below, men/women, large/small) based on union (alliance, companionship, marriage) and separation (the taboo of contact, of misalliance, etc.), symbolic capital is attached to groups – or to the names of groups, families, clans, tribes – and is both the instrument and the stakes of collective strategies seeking to conserve or increase it as well as individual strategies seeking to acquire or conserve it, by joining groups which possess it (through the exchange of gifts, companionship, marriage, etc.) and by distinguishing themselves from groups which possess little or are destitute (stigmatized ethnic groups).[8] One of the dimensions of symbolic capital, in differentiated societies, is ethnic identity which, with names or skin color, is a *percipi*, a being-perceived, functioning as positive or negative symbolic capital.

Since structures of perception and appreciation are essentially the product of the incorporation of objective structures, the structure of the distribution of symbolic capital tends to present a rather great stability. And symbolic revolutions imply a more or less radical revolution in instruments of knowledge and categories of perception.[9]

Thus, the precapitalist economy rests fundamentally on a denial of what we consider to be the economy, which obliges agents to keep implicit a certain number of operations and representations of those operations. The second, correlative property is the transfiguration of economic acts into symbolic acts, a transfiguration which can take place in practice as, for example, an exchange of gifts, where the gift ceases to be a material object to become a sort of message or symbol suited to creating a social link. The third property: in this circulation of a quite particular type, a specific form of capital is produced and accumulated, a form of capital which I have called symbolic capital and which appears in the social relations between properties possessed by an agent and other agents endowed with adequate categories of perception. A being-perceived constructed according to particular categories of perception, symbolic capital assumes the existence of social agents whose modes of thought are constituted in such a way that they know and recognize what is proposed to them, and that they believe in it, which means, in certain cases, obedience or submission.

The Taboo of Calculation

The constitution of the economy as an economy, which took place progressively in European societies, was accompanied by the negative constitution of small islands of precapitalist economy which live on in the universe of the economy constituted as such. This process corresponds to the emergence of a field, of a playing field, site of a new type of game, whose principle is the law of material interest. At its core a universe is established in which the law of the exchange of exact equivalents becomes the explicit rule and can be expressed *publicly*, in an almost cynical manner. For example, in business, the laws of the family are suspended. It does not matter that you are my cousin, I treat you like any buyer; there is no preference, privilege, exception, exemption. For the Kabyle, the moral codes of business, of the market, are opposed to the moral code of good faith, that of the *bu niya* (the man of good faith, of innocence, the man of honor), which excludes, for example, lending to a family member with interest. The market is the place of calculation or even diabolical ruse, the diabolical transgression of the sacred. Contrary to everything demanded by the economy of symbolic goods, there one can call a spade a spade, an interest an interest, a profit a profit. Gone is the work of euphemization which, among the Kabyle, was imposed even on the market: relations of the market themselves were immersed (*embedded*, as Polanyi says) in social relations (one does not trade in just any way and with just anyone; in sales or purchases, buyers and vendors surround themselves with guarantors, chosen among acquaintances of high repute because of their honor). The logic of the market only became autonomized very gradually, somehow extracting itself from that entire network of social relations of more or less enchanted dependence.

At the end of this process, through an effect of reversal, the domestic economy became the exception. Max Weber says somewhere that the passage is from societies in which economic affairs are conceived according to the model of kinship relations to societies where kinship relations themselves are conceived according to the model of economic relations. The spirit of calculation which was constantly repressed (even if the temptation of calculation was never absent, among the Kabyle or elsewhere) is progressively asserted as the conditions favorable to its exercise and its *public affirmation* are developed. The emergence of the economic field marks the appearance of a universe in which social agents can admit to themselves and admit publicly that they have interests and can tear themselves away from collective misrecognition; a universe in which they not only can do business, but can also admit to themselves that they are there to do business, that is, to conduct themselves in a self-interested manner, to calculate, make a profit, accumulate, and exploit.[10]

With the constitution of the economy and the generalization of monetary exchanges and the spirit of calculation, the domestic economy ceases to furnish the model of all other economic relations. Threatened in its specific logic by the market economy, it increasingly tends to affirm explicitly its specific logic, that of love. Taking the opposition to the limit through the clarity of demonstration, one can thus oppose the logic of domestic sexual exchanges, which have no price, and the logic of the market sexual relations, which have an explicit market price and are sanctioned by monetary exchanges. Housewives, who have no material utility or price (the taboo of calculation and credit), are excluded from market circulation (exclusivity) and are objects and subjects of feeling; in contrast, so-called venal women (prostitutes) have an explicit market price, based on money and calculation, are neither object nor subject of feeling and sell their body as an object.[11]

We see that, contrary to economistic reductionism à la Gary Becker,[12] who reduces to economic calculation that which by definition denies and defies calculation, the domestic unit manages to perpetuate in its core a quite particular economic logic. The family, as an integrated unit, is threatened by the logic of the economy. A monopolistic grouping defined by the exclusive appropriation of a determinate kind of goods (land, the family name, etc.), it is at the same time united and divided by property. The logic of the prevailing economic universe introduces, within the family, the rot of calculation, which undermines sentiments. United by patrimony, the family is the site of competition for that patrimony, and for power over it. But this competition continually threatens to destroy that capital by ruining the basis of its perpetuation, that is, unity, cohesion, integration; and it thus imposes behaviors intended to perpetuate the patrimony by perpetuating the unity of its heirs, who are divided about it. In the case of Algeria, I was able to show that the generalization of monetary exchanges and the correlative constitution of the "economic" idea of work as paid labor – in opposition to work as an occupation or a function which is an end in itself – leads to the generalization of calculating dispositions, threatening the indivisibility of goods and tasks on which the family unit rests. In fact, in differentiated societies, the spirit of calculation and the logic of markets undermine the spirit of solidarity and tend to substitute the individual decisions of the isolated individual for the collective decisions of the household or the head of the household and to favor the development of markets separated according to different categories of age or gender (teenagers) which make up households.

It would be necessary to recall here the analysis of the system of strategies of reproduction, strategies which are found, in different forms and with different relative weights, in all societies, and whose basis is this sort of *conatus*, the unconscious desire of the family or the household to perpetuate itself by perpetuating its unity against divisive factors, and especially against those inherent in competition for the property that underlies family unity.

As a group endowed with an esprit de corps (and destined, in this sense, to serve as an archetypal model for all social groups functioning as a corporate body – for example, the fraternities and sororities at American universities), the family is subject to two contradictory systems of forces: on the one hand the forces of the economy which introduce the tensions, contradictions and conflicts I have evoked, but which, in certain contexts, also impose the maintenance of a certain cohesion, and, on the other hand, the forces of cohesion which are in part linked to the fact that the reproduction of capital in its different forms depends, to a large degree, on the reproduction of the family unit.

This is true especially of symbolic capital and social capital which can only be reproduced through the reproduction of the primary social unit which is the family. Thus, in Kabylia, many families which had broken the unity of goods and tasks chose to present a facade of indivisibility in order to safeguard the honor and prestige of the great, united family. In the same sense, in the great bourgeois families of advanced modern societies, and even in the categories of employers furthest from the family mode of reproduction, economic agents make considerable room in their strategies and in their economic practices for the reproduction of enlarged domestic ties, which is one of the conditions for the reproduction of their capital. The rich and powerful have large families (which is, I believe, a general anthropological law); they have a specific interest in maintaining extended family relations and, through these relations, a particular form of concentration of capital. In other words, despite all the divisive forces exerted on it, the family remains one of the sites for the accumulation, conservation and reproduction of different kinds of capital. Historians know that great families survive revolutions (as the work of Chaussinand-Nogaret, among others, shows). A very extended family has very diversified capital, such that, provided that family cohesion lives on, survivors can mutually assist each other in the restoration of their collective capital.

At the very heart of the family, therefore, there is a work of reproduction of the domestic unit, of its integration, a work encouraged and sustained by institutions such as the Church (one would need to verify whether the essential element of what is included under the name of *morality* – especially Christian, but also lay – is not based on the unitary vision of the family) or the state. The latter contributes to establishing or reinforcing the category of construction of reality which is the idea of the family[13] through institutions such as the family registry, family benefits, and the whole set of actions which are at once symbolic and material, often accompanied by economic sanctions, which have the effect of reinforcing in each of its members the interest in maintaining the domestic unit. This action by the state is not simple and we would need to refine it, taking into consideration, for example, the antagonism between *civil law*, which often acts toward division – the civil code has posed considerable problems for the Béarnais, who have had great difficulty in perpetuating the family based on primogeniture within the limits of the juridical code which demands division in equal shares, and who have had to invent all sorts of tricks to get around the law and perpetuate the household against the forces of disruption introduced by the law – and *social law*, which privileges certain categories of family (for example, single-parent families) or which gives the sanction of the universal rule, through assistance, to a particular vision of the family, treated as a "natural" family.

We would still need to analyze the logic of exchanges between generations, a particular case of the economy of symbolic exchanges within the family. To attempt to account for the inability of relations of private contracts to assure the intertemporal allocation of resources, economists have constructed what they call models of overlapping generations: there are two categories of agents, the young and the old; the young at time t will be old at $t + 1$, the old at time t will have disappeared at $t + 1$, and there will be a new generation. How can the young transfer in time a part of the wealth they produce in order to consume it when they are old? Economists are interesting because they have a genius for imaginary variation, in Husserl's sense of the term, and they construct formal models which they make function in the abstract, thus providing formidable instruments to shatter the obvious and force one to question things that are taken for granted, even when one thinks one is being very paradoxical.

Economists support their analysis of intergenerational relations by arguing that money is indispensable and that its constancy over time is what enables the young to use the money they accumulate today when they are old, because the young of the following period will always accept it. Which amounts to saying (as does Simiand) that currency is always fiduciary and that its validity is based on a chain of durable beliefs over time. But in order for intergenerational exchanges to continue despite everything, the logic of debt as recognition must also intervene and a feeling of obligation or gratitude must be constituted. Relations between generations are one of the sites par excellence of the transfiguration of the recognition of debt into recognition, filial devotion, love. (Exchanges always follow the logic of the gift, not of credit, and loans between parents and children exclude the charging of interest, with repayment dates left vague.) Today, with *philia* being threatened by a breakdown of cohabitation brought about by work-related migration and by the generalization of the (necessarily egotistical) spirit of calculation, the state has taken over the management of exchanges between generations from the domestic unit. "Senior citizenship" is one of the collective inventions which has permitted the transferral of the management of the elderly previously vested in the family to the state, or, more precisely, which has replaced direct management of intergenerational exchanges within the family with the management of these exchanges assured by the state, which collects and redistributes resources destined for the elderly (another example of a case where the state brings a solution to the problem of the "free rider").

The Pure and the Commercial

I now turn to the economy of cultural goods, where we find most of the characteristics of the precapitalist economy. First, the denial of the economy: the genesis of an artistic field or a literary field is the progressive emergence of an economic world reversed, in which the positive sanctions of the market are indifferent or even negative.[14] The bestseller is not automatically recognized as a legitimate work, and commercial success may even mean condemnation. Inversely, the "accursed artist" or *artiste maudit* (who is a historical invention: he hasn't always existed, no more than the very idea of the artist) can draw from his malediction in this century the signs of election in the future. This vision of art (which is losing ground today as fields of cultural production lose their autonomy) was invented gradually, with the idea of the pure artist having no other objective than art itself, indifferent to the sanctions of the market, to official recognition, to success, as a quite particular social world was instituted, a small island in an ocean of interest, in which economic failure could be associated with a form of success, or, in any case, not appear as an irreparable failure. (This is one of the problems of unrecognized ageing artists who have to convince others and be convinced themselves that their failure is success and that they have a reasonable chance of success because theirs is a universe where the possibility of success without selling books, without being read, without being played, etc., is recognized.)

Thus, it is an upside-down world where negative sanctions can become positive sanctions; where, obviously, the truth of prices is systematically excluded. All language is euphemistic. Consequently, one of the major difficulties sociology encounters concerns the choice of words: if you say "producer," you sound reductionist and you effectively make the specificity of this space of production, which is not a form of production like the others, disappear; if you say "creator," you fall into the ideology of "creation," into the mystique of the unique artist, escaping science by definition, an ideology so powerful that it suffices to adopt it to look like an artist, and obtain all kinds of symbolic profits. (You write in a newspaper: "I, a creator, despise reductionist sociologists," etc., you pass for an artist; or a philosopher ... This is one of the reasons why a day does not go by without some newspaper, weekly, or magazine denouncing "the empire of the sociologist," the "sociologist-king," "the territory of the sociologist," etc.) This extremely powerful professional ideology is inscribed in language which excludes the vocabulary of the market economy: the art dealer calls herself a gallery director; publisher is a euphemism for book dealer, or buyer of literary labor (in the nineteenth century, writers often compared themselves to prostitutes . . .). The relationship between the avant-garde publisher and the author is quite similar to the relationship between the priest and the sacristan which I will soon describe. The publisher says to a young writer at the end of a difficult month, "Look at Beckett, he has never touched a penny of his royalties!" And the poor writer feels ashamed, he is not sure he's a Beckett, but he is sure that unlike Beckett he is base enough to ask for money . . . Or one can reread Flaubert's *Sentimental Education*: Mr Arnoux is a very ambiguous personage of the art market, half dealer, half artist, who has a half-sentimental, half-employer relationship with artists. These soft relations of exploitation only work if they are soft. They are relations of symbolic violence which can only be established with the complicity of those who suffer from it, like intradomestic relations. The dominated collaborate in their own exploitation through affection or admiration.

The artist's capital is a symbolic capital, and nothing more resembles the struggles for honor among the Kabyle than intellectual struggles. In many of those struggles, the apparent stake (to be right, to triumph through reason) hides the stakes of the point of honor. And this is true from the most frivolous (in the battles to know what is happening in Sarajevo, is the real stake Sarajevo?) to the most "serious" (as in quarrels for priority). This symbolic capital of recognition is a *percipi* which assumes the belief of those engaged in the field. This is what Duchamp has clearly shown – as has Karl Kraus in another context – in his veritable sociological experiments. By exhibiting a urinal in a museum, he revealed the constitutive effect which grants consecration through a consecrated space as well as the social conditions of the appearance of that effect. All the conditions are not reduced to these, but this act had to be carried out by him, that is, by a painter recognized as a painter and by other agents of the art world having the power to say who is a painter; it had to take place in a museum that recognized him as a painter and that had the power to recognize his act as an artistic act; the artistic milieu had to be ready to recognize that type of questioning of its recognition. Suffice to observe, *a contrario*, what happened with an artistic movement such as Arts Incohérents.[15] They were artists who carried out, at the end of the nineteenth century, a whole series of artistic acts which were redone in a very similar fashion in the 1960s, especially by conceptual artists. Since the "collective expectations" of which Mauss speaks did not exist, and "minds, as they say, were not prepared," they were not taken seriously – besides, partly because they did not take themselves seriously, they could not, given the state of the field, give and take as artistic acts what they no doubt considered mere dauber's jokes. One might therefore very well say, retrospectively: look, they invented everything! That is both true and false, because questions of precursors and precedents must be treated with great prudence. The social conditions for such artists to appear and appear to be doing what they seemed to do in our eyes were not fulfilled. Thus, they did not do it. Which means, for Duchamp to be Duchamp, the field had to be constituted in such a way that he could be Duchamp . . .

We would still need to extend all that has been said about symbolic capital as it functions in other universes to the writer's or artist's symbolic capital, to the fetishism of the author's name and the magical effect of the signature: as a *percipi*, it rests on belief, that is, on the categories of perception and appreciation in force in the field.

In dissociating temporal success and specific consecration and in assuring the specific profits of disinterestedness to those who submit to its rules, the artistic (or scientific) field creates the conditions for the constitution (or emergence) of a veritable interest in disinterestedness (equivalent to the interest in generosity of societies of honor). In the artistic world as an economic world reversed, the most anti-economic "follies" are in certain respects "reasonable" since in them disinterestedness is recognized and rewarded.

The Laughter of Bishops

The religious enterprise obeys, essentially, the principles I have drawn from the analysis of the precapitalist economy. As in the domestic economy, of which it is a transfigured form (with the model of fraternal exchange), the paradoxical character of the economy of the offering, of volunteerism, of sacrifice, is revealed in a particularly visible manner in the case of today's Catholic Church. In effect, this enterprise with an economic dimension founded on the denial of the economy is immersed in a universe where, with

the generalization of monetary exchanges, the search for the maximization of profit has become the basis of most ordinary practices, such that every agent – religious or nonreligious – tends to
evaluate in money, at least implicitly, the value of his or her work
or time in monetary terms. A sacristan or a beadle is a more or
less repressed *homo oeconomicus*; he knows that putting flowers
on the altar takes half an hour and that at the rate of a cleaning
woman it is worth a certain amount. But, at the same time, he
plays the religious game and would reject the comparison of his
work of religious service to that of a cleaning man or woman.

This sort of double consciousness, which is undoubtedly common to all social agents who participate both in the economic
universe and in one of the anti-economic sub-universes (we might
think of party activists and of all "volunteer workers"), is at the
basis of a very great (partial) lucidity which is manifested above
all in situations of crisis and among people in a precarious position, and thus out of synch with the most obvious and basic facts
of doxa. It is in this way that the magazine *Trait-d'union*, which
was created by nonreligious personnel of the Church when they
founded a kind of union to attempt to obtain material recognition
for the religious services they provided, is a formidable instrument
of analysis. The fact remains that to bring a form of behavior brutally back to its "economic" truth (to say that the chair attendant
is a cleaning woman without a salary) is to undertake a necessary,
but mystifying, demystification. The objectification makes it clear
that the Church is also an economic enterprise; but it risks making us forget that it is an economic enterprise that can only function as it does because it is not really a business, because it *denies*
that it is a business. (In the same sense that the family can only
function because it denies that it obeys the definition given it by
economism à la Gary Becker.)

Here again we find the problem which is provoked by the
making explicit of the truth of institutions (or fields) whose truth
is the avoidance of rendering their truth explicit. Put more simply:
rendering explicit brings about a destructive alteration when the
entire logic of the universe rendered explicit rests on the taboo of
rendering it explicit. Thus, I have been very struck by the fact
that each time the bishops used the language of objectification in
relation to the economy of the Church, speaking for example, of
a "phenomenon of supply and demand" to describe the pastoral,

they would laugh. (An example: "We are not societies, uh . . . quite like the others: we produce nothing, and we sell nothing [laughter], right?" – Chancery of the Paris diocese.) Or, at other moments, they invented extraordinary euphemisms. This leads one to think that one is witnessing not a cynical lie, as a Voltairean reading would have it, but rather a gap between the objective truth, repressed rather than ignored, and the lived truth of practices, and that this lived truth, which hides, through agents themselves, the truth brought to light by analysis, is part of the truth of practices in their complete definition. The truth of the religious enterprise is that of having two truths: economic truth and religious truth, which denies the former. Thus, in order to describe each practice, as among the Kabyle, it would be necessary to use two words, superimposed on each other as if in a musical chord: apostolate/marketing, faithful/clientele, sacred service/paid labour, and so forth. The religious discourse which accompanies practice is an integral part of the economy of practices as an economy of symbolic goods.

This ambiguity is a very general property of the *economy of the offering*, in which exchange is transfigured into self-sacrifice to a sort of transcendental entity. In most societies, one does not offer raw material to the divinity, gold for example, but rather polished gold. The effort to transfigure the raw material into a beautiful object, into a statue, is part of the work of euphemization of the economic relationship (which explains the interdiction of melting statues into gold). Jacques Gernet provides a very beautiful analysis of sacred commerce and of the Buddhist temple as a sort of bank – denied as such – which accumulates sacred resources, gifts, and offerings based on free consent and volunteerism, and profane benefits, like those sought by usurious or mercenary practices (loans of cereals, collateral loans, taxes on mills, taxes on products of the land, and so forth).[16] These resources, which are not used for the support of members of religious orders or buildings, or for worship services, feasts, official ceremonies, services for the dead, and so on, are accumulated as if in an "inexhaustible Treasury" and partially redistributed in the form of gifts to the poor or the sick or as free lodging for the faithful. Thus, the temple functions objectively as a sort of bank, but one which cannot be perceived and thought of as such, in fact, provided that it is never understood as such.

The religious enterprise is an enterprise with an economic dimension which cannot admit to so being and which functions in a sort of permanent negation of its economic dimension: I undertake an economic act, but I do not want to know it; I do it in such a way that I can tell myself and others that it is not an economic act – and I can be credible to others only if I believe it myself. The religious enterprise, the religious business, "is not an industrial and commercial enterprise with a lucrative objective," as *Trait-d'union* reminds us, that is, an enterprise like the others.[17] The problem of knowing whether this is cynical or not disappears completely if one sees that it forms part of the very conditions of its functioning and of the success of the religious enterprise, that religious agents believe in what they are doing and that they do not accept the strict economic definition of their action and their function. Thus, when the union of the Church's lay personnel attempted to define their professions, it ran up against the implicit definition of those professions defended by their employers (that is, the bishops who, obviously, reject this designation). Sacred tasks are irreducible to a purely economic and social codification: the sacristan does not have a "trade"; he renders a divine service. Here again the ideal definition defended by church dignitaries is part of the truth of practice.

This structural double game with the objective definition of practice is seen in the most ordinary forms of behavior. Thus, for example, near Saint-Sulpice there is a pilgrimage enterprise which is in fact (this is objectively, from the point of view of the observer, who reduces and dissipates the clouds of euphemistic discourses) a tourism business, but denied as such through a systematic usage of euphemism: a trip to England will be a "discovery of ecumenicalism"; a trip to Palestine, a "cruise with a religious theme, following in the steps of St Paul"; a trip to Russia, a "reencounter with orthodoxy." The transfiguration is essentially verbal: to be able to do what one does by making people (and oneself) believe that one is not doing it, one must tell them (and oneself) that one is doing something other than what one is doing, one must do it while saying (to oneself and others) that one is not doing it, as if one were not doing it.

Another example, the Chantiers du Cardinal, an enterprise responsible for the construction of French religious buildings: administered by a cleric, it employs a very important volunteer staff of retired engineers, law professors, and so forth, who donate their time and competence to the enterprise free of charge, and a very small number of paid employees who do exacting work, such as secretarial work or accounting, and who are preferably Catholic and thus recruited through cooptation, although they are not explicitly required to be Catholic. The chancery, which is the episcopate's ministry of finance, included (at the time of the survey) about 60 volunteers, primarily retirees. This structure – a small number of clerics, assisted by a small number of paid employees, supervising a large number of volunteers – is typical of Catholic enterprises. We find it everywhere, in the religious press, publishing, etc. Besides *volunteer work*, the free gift of labor and services, we also find here another central property of Catholic enterprise: it is always conceived of as a *large family*. There is a cleric, sometimes two, whose specific culture, tied to a whole collective and individual history, consists of knowing how to *manage* at the same time a vocabulary or a language and social relations, which must always be euphemized. Thus, what makes an educational establishment remain catholic, even if there is no longer a crucifix on the wall, is that there is an orchestra conductor who has profoundly incorporated this sort of catholic disposition or language, and a very particular way of managing relations between people.

In the religious enterprise, relations of production function according to the model of family relations: to treat others as brothers is to put the economic dimension of the relationship into parentheses. Religious institutions work permanently, both practically and symbolically, to euphemize social relations, including relations of exploitation (as in the family), by transfiguring them into relations of spiritual kinship or of religious exchange, through the logic of volunteerism. Alongside paid workers and subaltern religious agents – for example those who clean churches or who maintain and decorate the altars – there are those who give the gift of labor, "a freely granted offering of money and time."[18] Exploitation is *masked*: in discussions between bishops and union agents, the former constantly play on the ambiguity of sacred tasks; they attempt to make the latter admit that consecrated actions are consecrating, that religious acts are ends in themselves and that those who carry them out are rewarded by the very fact of carrying them out, that they are on the order of finality without end.

The functioning of the logic of volunteer work, and the exploitation it authorizes, are favored and facilitated by the objective ambiguity of sacred tasks: to push a wheelchair in a pilgrimage is at once a charitable act which is its own end, and which merits reward in the hereafter, and a technical act that could be carried out by a paid nurse. Is maintenance of the place of worship a technical act or a ritual act (of purification)? And the manufacture of an effigy (I am thinking of interviews I had with workers who paint statues of the Virgin in Lourdes)? The function of agents is no less ambiguous: the sacristan prepares religious services and maintains the places of worship; he is responsible for preparing baptisms, weddings, and funeral ceremonies; he assists in these different ceremonies and looks after parish locales. His activity is a ritual service (even if he himself is not consecrated). The paper *Trait-d'union* speaks of the "religious finality of labor."[19]

When lay personnel fulfill *profane* functions such as those of telephone operator, secretary, or accountant, and formulate *demands*, they run up against the clerics' tendency to consider their responsibility as a privilege or a sacred duty. (Volunteer work is above all done by women, for whom, at least in certain categories, the equivalence of work and its value in money is not clearly established; and the sacerdotal corps, which is masculine, uses established forms of the division of labour between the sexes to demand and accept free services.) When sacristans recall that there is a religious finality to their work, but that it does not necessarily mean, therefore, that the work does not merit a salary, bishops respond that salary is a word that does not have a place in this universe. In the same way, to a researcher who asks, somewhat clumsily ("gaffs" can be very revealing, in that they often shatter that which seems obvious), if "for Monsignor Untel, going to Aix is a promotion," an important member of the episcopate's secretariat responds: "Oh yes, of course, it is even a bit surprising, it is like X who went from auxiliary in Nancy, which is still a large diocese, to Bishop of Cambrai . . . Said in this way, it is certainly true, but we do not really like the term promotion. We would rather say recognition." Another example of sacerdotal clarification about salaries:

First, the priest does not receive a salary, that's the first thing! I think that is important, because whoever says salary says wage

earner, and the priest is not a wage earner. Between the priest and
the bishop there is a contract, if you wish, but it is a *sui generis*
contract, a quite special contract, which is not a contract for
services, between employer and employee . . . But here, we cannot
say that there is a salary. Priests are not wage earners; we cannot
speak of honoraria, but we can speak of a special treatment, if you
wish, that is taken care of by the bishop. What is the contract
between the priest and the bishop? The priest pledges his entire
life to the Church and, in exchange, the bishop commits to providing for his needs . . . We can speak of special treatment, if you
wish, in the very broad sense, but I would put it in quotation
marks. But there is no salary! No salary!

Quotation marks are one of the most powerful markers of negation and of passage to the order of the symbolic economy.

Clerics themselves also have an ambiguous economic status, as
they live in misrecognition: they are poor (they receive the guaranteed minimum wage), but their poverty is only apparent (they
receive all sorts of gifts) and is elective (their resources come in
the form of offerings, gifts; they are dependent on their clientele).
This structure suits a double habitus, endowed with the genius
of euphemism, of ambiguous practices and discourses, of double
meanings without a double game. The director of pilgrimages for
the Paris region speaks of the organization of "spiritual activities"
in relation to Lourdes. When he speaks of a "clientele," he laughs
as if hearing a dirty word. Religious language functions permanently as an instrument of euphemization. It suffices to let it flow,
to let flow the automatisms inscribed in the religious habitus, of
which language is an essential dimension. This structural duplicity,
which leads to double-edged strategies – permitting the accumulation of religious profit and economic profit – and a double
language, could be one of the invariables of the personage of the
proxy (priest, delegate, politician) of a Church or a party.

We are thus dealing with enterprises (educational, medical,
charity, etc.) which, functioning according to the logic of volunteer
work and offering, have a considerable advantage in economic
competition (among these advantages, the effect of the label: the
adjective "Christian" having the value of a guarantee of quasi-
domestic morality). But these objectively economic enterprises can
only benefit from these advantages provided that the conditions

of the *misrecognition* of their economic dimension are continually reproduced, that is, as long as agents succeed in believing and making others believe that their actions have no economic impact.

We can thus understand how essential it is, from the methodological point of view, to avoid dissociating economic functions and religious functions, that is, the properly economic dimension of practice and the symbolism that makes the fulfillment of economic functions possible. Discourse is not something additional (as some tend to lead one to believe when they speak of "ideology"); it is part of the economy itself. And, if one wants to be precise, it must be taken into consideration, along with the efforts apparently spent in the work of euphemization: religious work includes a considerable expenditure of energy aimed at converting activity with an economic dimension into a sacred task; one must accept wasting time, making an effort, even suffering, in order to believe (and make others believe) that one is doing something other than what one is doing. There is a loss, but the law of conservation of energy remains true because that which is lost is recovered in another position.

What is valid at the lay level is true to the nth degree for the level of the clerics who are always in the logic of *self-deception*. But to speak of self-deception may lead one to believe that each agent is responsible for deceiving himself. In fact, the work of self-deception is a collective work, sustained by a whole set of social institutions of assistance, the first and most powerful of which is language, which is not only a means of expression, but also a principle of structuration functioning with the support of a group which benefits from it: collective bad faith is inscribed in the objectivity of language (in particular in euphemisms, ritual formulae, terms of address – "my father," "my sister," etc. – and reference), of liturgy, of the social technology of the catholic administration of exchanges and social relations (for example, all the organizational traditions) and also in the bodies, the habitus, the ways of being, of speaking, and so forth; it is permanently reinforced by the logic of the economy of symbolic goods which encourages and rewards this structural duplicity. For example, the logic of "fraternal" relations is inscribed in socially instituted dispositions, but also in traditions and places: there is a whole series of magazines called *Dialogue* or which call for "dialogue," there are dialogue professionals who can dialogue with the most different kinds of people using the most different languages, there are meeting places, and so forth.

Finally, I have already outlined elsewhere[20] an analysis of the economy of public goods and of the bureaucratic field, of the state, as one of the sites of the denial of the economy. (As a parenthesis, it is important to know that the Church has long fulfilled quasi-state functions of general interest and public service; it achieved the first *concentration of public capital* dedicated to public ends – education, care of the sick, of orphans, etc., which explains why it entered into very violent competition with the state at the moment when the "social" state was put into place, in the nineteenth century.) The order of the "public," of "public matters," was historically constituted through the emergence of a field where acts of general interest, of public service, were possible, encouraged, known, recognized and rewarded. The fact remains that this bureaucratic field has never succeeded in obtaining dedication from its agents as complete as that obtained by the family (or even the Church) and that service in the interests of the state is always in competition with service for personal or family interests. Public law should recall that "administration does not give presents." And, in fact, an administrative action which benefits a private individual in an individualized manner is suspect, indeed illicit.

I still must explain the principles of the logic that the different universes that I have briefly described have in common.

The economy of symbolic goods rests on the repression or the censorship of economic interests (in the narrow sense of the term). As a consequence, economic truth, that is, the price, must be actively or passively hidden or left vague. The economy of symbolic goods is an economy of imprecision and indeterminacy. It is based on a taboo of making things explicit (a taboo which analysis violates, by definition, thus exposing itself to making seem calculating and interested practices which are defined against calculation and interest).

Because of this repression, the strategies and practices characteristic of the economy of symbolic goods are always ambiguous, two-sided, and even apparently contradictory (for example, goods have a price and are "priceless"). This duality of mutually exclusive truths, as much in practices as in discourse (euphemism), should not be thought of as duplicity, hypocrisy, but rather as denial assuring (through a sort of *Aufhebung*) the coexistence of opposites (one can attempt to account for it through the metaphor of the musical chord: apostolate/marketing, faithful/clients, worship/work, production/creation, etc.).

The work of denial or repression can only succeed because it is collective and based on the orchestration of the habitus of those who accomplish it or, in simpler terms, on an unintentionally concluded or concerted agreement between the dispositions of the agents directly or indirectly concerned. The economy of symbolic exchanges rests not on the logic of rational action or of *common knowledge* (I know that you know that I know that you will reciprocate) which leads one to think of the most characteristic actions of this economy as contradictory or impossible, but rather on *shared misrecognition* (I am the way I am, disposed in such a way that I know and do not want to know that you know and do not want to know that I know and do not want to know that you will give me a countergift). The collective work of repression is only possible if agents are endowed with the same categories of perception and appreciation. In order for the double-faced relation between the elder brother and the younger brother to function durably, as in Béarnaise society of old, the younger brother's submission and his devotion to the interests of the lineage – the "family spirit" – must be joined by the elder brother's generosity and tactfulness, the basis of his attention and consideration toward his brother, and, among all others, in the family or outside of it, by similar dispositions which make identical forms of behavior be approved and symbolically rewarded.

These common dispositions, and the shared doxa they establish, are the product of an identical or similar socialization leading to the generalized incorporation of the structures of the market of symbolic goods in the form of cognitive structures in agreement with the objective structures of that market. Symbolic violence rests on the adjustment between the structures constitutive of the habitus of the dominated and the structure of the relation of domination to which they apply: the dominated perceive the dominant through the categories that the relation of domination has produced and which are thus identical to the interests of the dominant.

Because the economy of symbolic goods is based on belief, the principle of its reproduction or crisis is found in the reproduction or crisis of belief, that is, in continuity or rupture with the adjustment between mental structures (categories of perception and appreciation, systems of preference) and objective structures. But the rupture cannot result from a simple awakening of consciousness; the transformation of dispositions cannot occur without a prior or concomitant transformation of the objective structures of which they are the product and which they can survive.

Notes

1 See Pierre Bourdieu, *The Logic of Practice*, trans. Richard Nice (Cambridge: Polity Press, 1990), pp. 105–7.
2 Ibid., p. 112.
3 Ibid., pp. 189–90 (on the sense of honor, or *nif*).
4 Cf. V. Zelizer, *Pricing the Priceless Child* (New York: Basic Books, 1987); *The Social Meaning of Money* (New York: Basic Books, 1994).
5 See Bourdieu, *The Logic of Practice*, p. 191.
6 "L'Économie de la maison," *Actes de la Recherche en Sciences Sociales*, nos 81–2 (Mar. 1990).
7 Pierre Bourdieu, "La domination masculine," *Actes de la Recherche en Sciences Sociales*, no. 84 (Sept. 1990), pp. 3–31.
8 Cf. the analysis of the functioning of salons in Proust: Bourdieu, *The Logic of Practice*, pp. 140–1.
9 See Pierre Bourdieu, *The Rules of Art: Genesis and Structure of the Literary Field* (Cambridge: Polity Press, 1996), pp. 170–1.
10 One can read Émile Benveniste's work, *Indo-European Language and Society* (London: Faber, 1973), as an analysis of the process through which the fundamental concepts of economic thought are progressively disengaged from the set of noneconomic meanings (family, political, religious, and so forth) in which they were immersed (for example, purchase and repurchase). As Lukács remarks (in *History and Class Consciousness* (Cambridge, Mass.: MIT Press, 1971), pp. 230–1), the progressive formation of political economy as an autonomous discipline, taking as its object the economy *as* economy, is itself a dimension of the process of autonomization of the economic field, which means that there are historical and social conditions of possibility of this science, which must be made explicit, at the risk of ignoring the limits of this so-called "pure theory."

11 According to Cecile Hoigard and Liv Finstad, numerous prostitutes say that, contrary to appearances, they prefer street prostitution, an expeditious sale of the body which allows a sort of mental reserve, to hotel prostitution which, insofar as it mimics – with a high degree of euphemization – free encounters, requires a greater expenditure of time and effort in pretending, of euphemization: in the first case, encounters are brief and rapid, during which they can think of something else and just act as objects; in contrast, hotel encounters, which appear to be more respectful of the person, are experienced as much more alienating because the prostitute must talk to the client, pretend to be interested in him, and the freedom in alienation which provides the possibility of thinking about something else disappears for the benefit of a relationship which recalls some of the ambiguity of nonmercenary love affairs (C. Hoigard and L. Finstad, *Backstreets: Prostitution, Money and Love* (University Park: Pennsylvania State University Press, 1992)).

12 See i.e. Gary S. Becker, *The Economic Approach to Human Behavior* (Chicago: University of Chicago Press, 1976).

13 Cf. "The Family Spirit," appendix to ch. 3 above.

14 See Bourdieu, *The Rules of Art*, pp. 141ff.

15 D. Grojnowski, "Une avant-garde sans avancée, les 'Arts incohérents', 1882–1889," *Actes de la Recherche en Sciences Sociales*, no. 40 (1981), pp. 73–86.

16 J. Gernet. *Les Aspects économiques du bouddhisme dans la société chinoise des Ve et Xe siècles* (Saigon: École Française d'Extrême-Orient, 1956).

17 *Trait-d'union*, no. 20, p. 20.

18 Ibid.

19 Ibid., no. 21, p. 1.

20 See pp. 59–60 and 90–1 above.

APPENDIX

Remarks on the Economy of the Church

First, the manifest image: an institution charged with assuring the salvation of souls. Or, at a higher degree of objectivization, with Max Weber: a (sacerdotal) corps holding the monopoly on the legitimate manipulation of the goods of salvation; and, for this reason, invested with a properly spiritual power, exercised *ex officio*, on the foundation of a permanent transaction with the expectations of the laity: the Church relies on principles of vision (dispositions which constitute "belief"), which it in part constituted, to orient representations or practices by reinforcing or transforming these principles. It can do this because of its relative autonomy in relation to the demands of the laity.

But the Church is also an enterprise with an economic dimension, capable of assuring its own perpetuation based on different kinds of resources. Here still, an apparent, official image: the Church lives from offerings or counterservices in exchange for its religious service (contributions to parish costs) and the revenues from its possessions (the Church's property). Reality is considerably more complex: the Church's temporal power also rests on its control of *positions* or jobs which may owe their existence to simple economic logic (when they are associated with economic enterprises with a properly religious function, such as pilgrimages, or with a religious dimension, such as the enterprises of the Catholic press) or to *state assistance*, such as teaching positions.

Those most directly affected often ignore the real economic bases of the Church, as evidenced by a typical declaration: "Since the state gives nothing to the Church, the faithful keep the Church alive through their offerings."[1] Nevertheless, the profound transformation of the Church's economic bases is expressed in the fact that those responsible for the institution can foreground the Church's material possessions, which previously were rigorously denied or dissimulated particularly when they were the principal target of anti-clerical criticism.

As a consequence of this transformation, in order to measure the Church's influence, one can now substitute the survey of practitioners and the intensity of their practice, such as that conducted by Canon Boulard, with a census of the positions whose *raison d'être* is the Church's existence and Christian belief and which would disappear if one or the other were themselves to disappear (this also applies to industries that make candles, chaplets, or religious images, as well as religious teaching establishments or the denominational press). This second measure is much more adequate: everything seems to indicate that we are moving toward a *Church without a faithful* whose strength (inseparably political and religious or, as is said in the language of clerics, "apostolic") rests on the ensemble of posts or jobs it holds.

The change in the economic foundations of the Church's existence, which has taken place gradually, relegates purely symbolic transactions with the laity (and the symbolic power exercised by preaching and the treatment of souls) to a second plane in relation to transactions with the state which assure the bases of the Church's temporal power, exercised through positions financed by the state, over agents who have to be Christians (Catholics) in order to occupy the positions it controls.

The Church's grip on a set of positions (teaching in a Catholic establishment, but also working as a guard at a pool associated with a religious establishment, serving as an administrator in a religious hospice, and so forth) which, without Catholic affiliation or practice being explicitly demanded, belong as a matter of priority to members of the Catholic community and encourage those who occupy them or who aspire to them to remain Catholic, secures the Church control of a sort of *state clientele* and, therefore, a revenue of material and, in any case, symbolic profits (and this without needing to secure for itself direct ownership of corresponding establishments with an economic dimension).

In this sense, the Church seems more like the image of disinterestedness and humility which conforms to its declared vocation.

Through a sort of inversion of ends and means, the defense of private teaching appears to be a defense of the indispensable means for the accomplishment of the Church's spiritual (pastoral, apostolic) function, while it seeks first to assure the Church the positions, the "Catholic" jobs which are the primary condition of its perpetuation and which the teaching activities are used to justify.[2]

Appendix Notes

1 *Radioscopie de l'Église en France, 1980, les 30 dossiers du service d'information de l'épiscopat pour le voyage de Jean-Paul II* (Paris: Bayard Presse, 1980), p. 27.
2 The rapprochement which often occurs between the Church and political parties (in particular the Communist Party) is thus grounded in this structural and functional homology. Like the Church, the party must maintain its control over the positions that it holds (in the different representative assemblies, in municipalities and all party, sports, and educational organizations) in order to maintain its control over those who hold them.

6

The Scholastic Point of View

I would like to organize my reactions to the remarks that have been addressed to me around three themes. First, I would like to analyze what I call, borrowing an expression of Austin, the "scholastic view," the point of view of the *skholè*, that is, the academic vision. What does our thinking owe to the fact that it is produced within an academic space? From there, I will try to give some indications on the particular problem that the understanding of practices poses and which makes for such a difficult task for the human sciences. Then, I would like to raise the issue of the relations between reason and history. Isn't sociology, which apparently undermines the foundations of reason and thereby its own foundations, capable of producing instruments for forging a rational discourse and even of offering techniques for waging a politics of reason, a realpolitik of reason?

Playing Seriously

"Scholastic view" is an expression that Austin uses in passing in *Sense and Sensibilia* (1962) and for which he gives an example: the particular use of language where, instead of grasping and mobilizing the meaning of a word that is immediately compatible with the situation, we mobilize and examine all the possible meanings of that word, outside of any reference to the situation. This very significant example contains the essentials of what the scholastic view is. The scholastic view is a very peculiar point of view on the social world, on language, on any possible object of thought that is made possible by the situation of *skholè*, of leisure, of which the school – a word which also derives from *skholè* – is a particular form, as an institutionalized situation of studious leisure. Adoption of this scholastic point of view is the admission fee tacitly demanded by all scholarly fields: the neutralizing disposition (in Husserl's sense), implying the bracketing of all theses of existence and all practical intentions, is the condition – at least as much as the possession of a specific competence – for access to museums and works of art. It is also the condition for the academic exercise as a gratuitous game, as a mental experience that is an end in and of itself.

We should take Plato's reflections on *skholè* very seriously and even his famous expression, so often commented upon, *spoudaiôs paizein*, "to play seriously." The scholastic point of view is inseparable from the scholastic situation, a socially instituted situation in which one can defy or ignore the common alternative between playing (*paizein*), joking, and being serious (*spoudazein*) by playing seriously and taking ludic things seriously, busying oneself with problems that serious, and truly busy, people ignore – actively or passively. *Homo scholasticus* or *homo academicus* is someone who can play seriously because his or her state (or State) assures her the means to do so, that is, free time, outside the urgency of a practical situation, the necessary competence assured by a specific apprenticeship based on *skholè*, and, finally but most importantly, the disposition (understood as an aptitude and an inclination) to invest and to invest oneself in the futile stakes, at least in the eyes of serious people, which are generated in scholastic worlds (serious people like Calliclès who, after having asked Socrates if he was joking or serious, made him remark that the serious games of philosophy carried the risk for those who, like himself, devoted themselves to it far beyond youth, that they would be cut off from everything that serious people take seriously).

To truly enter these universes where context-free practices or utterances are produced, one must dispose of time, of *skholè*, and also have this disposition to play gratuitous games which is acquired and reinforced by situations of *skholè*, such as the inclination and the ability to raise speculative problems for the sole pleasure of resolving them, and not because they are posed, often quite urgently, by the necessities of life, to treat language not as an instrument but as an object of contemplation, delight or speculation.

Thus, what philosophers, sociologists, historians, and all those whose profession it is to think and speak about the world have the greatest chance of overlooking are the social presuppositions inscribed in the scholastic point of view, what, to awaken philosophers from their scholastic slumber, I shall call by the oxymoron of *epistemic doxa*: thinkers leave in a state of unthought (*impensé*, doxa) the presuppositions of their thought, that is, the social conditions of possibility of the scholastic point of view and the unconscious dispositions, productive of unconscious theses, which are acquired through an academic or scholastic experience, often inscribed in prolongation of originary (bourgeois) experience of distance from the world and from the urgency of necessity.

In contradistinction with Plato's lawyer, or Cicourel's physician,[1] we have the time, all our time, and this freedom from urgency, from necessity – which often takes the form of economic necessity, due to the convertibility of time into money – is made possible by an ensemble of social and economic conditions, by the existence of these supplies of free time that accumulated economic resources represent (Weber notes in *Economy and Society* that the primary accumulation of political capital appears with the *notable* when the latter has amassed sufficient resources to be able to leave aside, for a time, the activity that provides his means of subsistence or to have somebody replace him).

This reminder of the economic and social conditions of the scholastic posture is not designed to condemn or to instill a guilt complex. The logic in which I reason is not that of condemnation or political denunciation, but that of epistemological questioning. This is a fundamental epistemological question since it bears on the epistemic posture itself, on the presuppositions inscribed in the fact of thinking the world, of retiring from the world and from action in the world in order to think that action. What we want to know is in what ways this withdrawal, this abstraction, this retreat impact on the thought that they make possible and thereby on what we think.

Thus, for instance, if it is true that the condition of possibility of everything that is produced in fields of cultural production is this sort of bracketing of temporal emergency and of economic necessity (as can easily be seen in the use of language: we do not use language to do something with it, we use language to raise questions about language), if it is true that we are in a universe which is that of gratuitousness, of finality without purpose, of aesthetics, is it not understandable that we should understand aesthetics so wrongly? Indeed – this is what I wanted to tell Jules Vuillemin yesterday[2] – there are questions that we do not ask of aesthetics because the social conditions of possibility of our aesthetic questioning are already aesthetic, because we forget to question all the nonthetic aesthetic presuppositions of all aesthetic theses . . .

Theory of the Theoretical Point of View

You may wonder why, being a sociologist, I should play the part of the philosopher. Partly, of course, it is in homage to my philosopher friends who have convened here. But it is also because I am *obliged* to do so. To raise such questions on the very nature of the scientific gaze is an integral part of scientific work. These questions have been thrust upon me, outside of any intent or taste for pure speculation, in a number of research situations where to understand my strategies or materials I was compelled to reflect upon the scholarly mode of knowledge. To the extent that it engages in a mode of thinking which presupposes the bracketing of practical necessity and the use of instruments of thought constructed against the logic of practice, such as game theory, the theory of probability, etc., the scholastic vision risks destroying its object or creating pure artifacts whenever it is applied without critical reflection to practices that are the product of an altogether different vision. Scholars who do not know what defines them as scholars from the "scholastic point of view" risk putting into the minds of agents *their* scholastic view or imputing to their object that which belongs to the manner of approaching it, to the mode of knowledge.

This epistemocentric fallacy can be found, for instance, in Chomsky, who operates as if ordinary speakers were grammarians. Grammar is a typical product of the scholastic point of view. Building on the work of Vygotsky, one could show that *skholè* is what allows us to move from primary mastery to secondary mastery of language, to accede to metadiscourse on the practice of discourse. The scholastic paralogism, the *scholastic fallacy*, consists in injecting *meta-* into discourses and practices. This is what Chomsky does; this is also what Lévi-Strauss does when he plays on the notion of *rule*, which Wittgenstein taught us to discern.

If, in studies of kinship, in Béarn or Kabylia, I was led to think of matrimonial practices as oriented by strategies rather than guided or directed by rules, it was not for some sort of philosophical point of honor, but rather to explain practices – with the help of theoretical analyses such as those of Wittgenstein, whom I just evoked. To speak of strategies rather than rules is to construct the object differently, to ask different questions of informants, to analyze marriages differently. Instead of being content with recording, via genealogies, marriages reduced to a kinship relation between spouses, I had to gather for each wedding all the data – and there are a lot of them – that may have entered, consciously or unconsciously, in the strategies: the age difference between spouses, differences in material or symbolic wealth between the two families, and so forth.

But to effect this radical conversion of the scientific gaze, we must take a theoretical point of view on the theoretical point of view; we must realize that the anthropologist is not, when faced with marriage, in the position of the head of the household who wishes to marry his daughter and to marry her well. The anthropologist (without knowing it) brackets all practical interests and stakes. This is rather obvious in the case of the ethnographer working in a foreign culture, whose situation as an outsider suffices to put him or her in a quasi-theoretical point of view. For the sociologist, however, it is much less obvious, and he can easily forget the gap that separates the interest that he may have in the school system as a scholar who simply wants to understand and to explain, and that consequently leads him to cast a "pure" gaze on the functioning of the mechanisms of differential elimination according to cultural capital, and the interest that he has in this same system when he acts as a father concerned with the future of his children. The notions of matrimonial strategy and of interest (the interest in maximizing the material or symbolic profits obtained through marriage) immediately come to mind when you start thinking as an agent acting within cultural traditions where the essential part of processes of accumulation or dilapidation of (economic or symbolic) capital work themselves out via matrimonial exchanges.

The same applies to myth or ritual, and in a way *a fortiori*. It is only on condition that we take up the point of view of practice – on the basis of a theoretical reflection on the theoretical point of view, as a nonpractical point of view, founded upon the neutralization of practical interests and practical stakes – that we have some chance of grasping the truth of the specific logic of practice. Ritual action, which structural anthropology situates on the side of algebra, is in fact a gymnastics or a dance (one goes from right to left, or from left to right, one throws over the left or the right shoulder) and follows a practical logic, that is, a logic that is intelligible, coherent, but only up to a certain point (beyond which it would no longer be "practical"), and oriented toward practical ends, that is, the actualization of wishes, or desires (of life or of death), etc.

Here again, the conversion in theoretical approach provoked by theoretical reflection on the theoretical point of view and on the practical point of view, and on their profound differences, is not purely speculative: it is accompanied by a drastic change in the practical operations of research and by quite tangible scientific profits. For instance, one is led to pay attention to properties of ritual practice that structuralist logicism would tend to push aside or to treat as meaningless aberrations of the mythical algebra: the ambiguities, the polysemic realities, underdetermined or indeterminate, not to speak of partial contradictions and the fuzziness that pervades the whole system and accounts for its flexibility, its openness, in short everything that makes it "practical" and thus geared to respond at the least cost (in particular in terms of logical research) to the emergencies of ordinary existence and practice.

One would need here to push the analysis further and to track down all the *scientific* mistakes which, in sociology as well as ethnology, derive from what could be called the *scholastic fallacy*, such as the fact of asking interviewees to be their own sociologists (as with all questions of the type: "According to you, how many social classes are there?") for lack of having questioned the questionnaire or, better, the situation of the questionnaire designer who has the leisure or the privilege to tear himself or herself away from the evidences of *doxa* to raise questions. Or worse: the fact of asking survey respondents questions to which they can always respond by yes or no but which they do not raise and could not ask themselves (that is, truly produce by themselves) unless they

were predisposed and prepared by the social conditions of existence to take up a "scholastic point of view" on the social world (as
in so many questions of political theory) and on their own practice. We would also need to uncover all the unnoticed theoretical
effects produced by the mere use of instruments of thought that,
having been produced in a "scholastic situation" – such as means
of recording, writing, transcription, as well as tools of "model-
ling," genealogies, diagrams, tables, and so forth – reproduce in
their functioning the presuppositions inscribed in the social conditions of their construction, such as the bracketing of time, of
temporal urgency, or the philosophy of gratuitousness, of the
neutralization of practical ends.

In short, to play on a famous title of Ryle's, I would say that
ignoring everything that is implicated in the "scholastic point of
view" leads to the most serious epistemological mistake in the
human sciences, namely, that which consists in putting "a scholar
inside the machine," in picturing all social agents in the image of
the scientist (of the scientist reasoning on human practice and not
of the acting scientist, the scientist in action) or, more precisely,
to place the models that the scientist must construct to account
for practices into the consciousness of agents, to operate as if the
constructions that the scientist must produce to understand and
account for practices were the main determinants, the actual cause
of practices. The rational calculator that the advocates of rational
action theory portray as the principle of human practices is no
less absurd – even if this does not strike us as much, perhaps
because it flatters our "spiritual point of honor" – than the *angelus
rector*, the far-seeing pilot to which some pre-Newtonian thinkers
attributed the regulated movement of the planets.

To "put a scholar inside the machine" is, thus, to risk falling
almost indifferently into finalistic intellectualism (of which I have
just given examples), or into mechanism or, as among the most
thoughtless scholars, to oscillate permanently between one and the
other. In fact, if I had the time I could show that a correct theory
of practices avoids these palinodes by making the very alternative that they conceal, and which Jacques Bouveresse has evoked,[3]
disappear: that of explanations based on causes and explanations
based on reasons or intentions. I will limit myself to one example.
In its apparent obscurity, the expression "noblesse oblige" clearly
states the specific logic of the *disposition*: the noble's habitus directs

(in the double sense of the word) his practices and thoughts like a force ("it is stronger than I"), but without mechanically constraining him; it also guides his action like a logic of necessity ("there is nothing else I can do," "I can do no differently"), but without imposing it on him as if it were a rule or as if he were submitting to the verdict in a sort of rational calculation. This leads me to believe that, in order to understand the specific logic of practices that have dispositions as their basis, we must abandon the canonical distinction between explanations based on causes and explanations based on reasons.

The Privilege of the Universal

When we unthinkingly put to work our most ordinary modes of thinking, we inflict upon our object a fundamental adulteration, which can go all the way to pure and simple *destruction* and that may well remain unnoticed. The same is true when we apply, beyond their conditions of historical and social validity (leading to anachronism or to class ethnocentrism), concepts that, as Kant puts it, seem to "pretend to universal validity" because they are produced in particular conditions whose particularity eludes us. How could we not see – to be more Kantian than Kant, and than my friend Jules Vuillemin – that the disinterested game of sensitiveness, the pure exercise of the faculty of feeling, in short, the so-called transcendental use of sensitivity, presupposes *historical and social conditions of possibility* and that aesthetic pleasure, this pure pleasure which "every person ought to be able to experience," is the privilege of those who have access to the conditions in which such a "pure" disposition can be durably constituted?

What do we do, for instance, when we talk of a "popular aesthetics" or when we want at all costs to credit the "people" (*le peuple*), who do not care to have one, with a "popular culture"? Forgetting to effect the *épochè* of the social conditions of the *épochè* of practical interests that we effect when we pass a pure aesthetic appreciation, we purely and simply universalize the particular case in which we are placed or, to speak a bit more roughly, we, in an unconscious and *thoroughly theoretical* manner, grant the economic and social privilege that is the precondition of the pure and universal aesthetic point of view to all men and women (and in particular to this good old peasant – evoked by Jules Vuillemin – who is capable of appreciating, like us, the beauty of a landscape, or to the black subproletarian capable of appreciating the rhythm or appeal of a rap melody).

Most of the human works that we are accustomed to treating as universal – law, science, the fine arts, ethics, religion, and so forth – cannot be dissociated from the scholastic point of view and from the social and economic conditions which make the latter possible. They have been engendered in these very peculiar social universes which are the fields of cultural production – the juridical field, the scientific field, the artistic field, the philosophical field – and in which agents are engaged who have in common the *privilege* of fighting for the monopoly of the universal, and thereby effectively of promoting the advancement of truths and values that are held, at each moment, to be universal, indeed eternal.

I am ready to concede that Kant's aesthetics is true, but only as a phenomenology of the aesthetic experiences of all those people who are the product of *skholè*. That is to say that the experience of the beautiful of which Kant offers us a rigorous description has definite economic and social conditions of possibility that are ignored by Kant, and that the anthropological possibility of which Kant sketches an analysis could become *truly universal* only if those economic and social conditions were universally distributed. It means also that the conditions of actual universalization of this (theoretical) universal possibility is thus the actual universalization of the economic and social conditions, that is, of *skholè*, which, being monopolized by some today, confer upon this happy few the monopoly over the universal.

To drive the point home and at the risk of appearing overly insistent – but in such matters, it is so easy to have a light touch – I would say that the *datum* from which sociological reflection starts is not the universal capacity to grasp the beautiful, but rather the incomprehension, the indifference of some social agents who are deprived of the adequate categories of aesthetic perception and appreciation. And to recall the social conditions of possibility of this judgment that claims universal validity leads us to circumscribe the pretentions to universality of Kantian analysis: we may grant the *Critique of Judgment* a limited validity as a phenomenological analysis of the lived experience of certain cultivated men and women in certain historical societies, and we can describe very precisely the genesis of this experience. But only to add immediately that the *unconscious universalization of the particular case* which it effects (by ignoring its own social conditions of possibility or, to be Kantian to the end, its own *limits*) has the effect of constituting a *particular* experience of the work of art (or of the world, as with the idea of "natural beauty") as a *universal norm* of all possible aesthetic experience, and thus of tacitly *legitimizing* a particular form of experience and, thereby, those who have the privilege of access to it.

What is true of pure aesthetic experience is true of all the anthropological possibilities that we tend to think of as (potentially) universal, such as the ability to produce a complex chain of logical reasoning or the ability to accomplish a perfectly rigorous moral act. And yet these abilities or capabilities remain the privilege of only a few because these anthropological potentialities find their full realization only under definite social and economic conditions; and because, inversely, there are economic and social conditions under which they are atrophied, annulled.

This is to say that one cannot, at the same time, denounce the inhuman social conditions of existence imposed upon proletarians and subproletarians, especially in the black ghettos of the United States and elsewhere, and credit the people placed in such situations with the full accomplishment of their human potentialities, and in particular with the gratuitous and disinterested dispositions that we tacitly or explicitly inscribe in notions such as those of "culture" or "aesthetics." The commendable concern to *rehabilitate* (which no doubt inspired me when I showed, a long time ago, that the photographs taken by members of the working class pursue an immanent intention which has its own coherence, its own logic, its own justification – which still does not entitle us to speak of an aesthetics) is not in itself a guarantee of comprehension, and it may end up yielding the opposite result. I understand Labov when he purports to show that the dialect of the residents of black ghettos can convey theological truths as subtle and sophisticated as do the knowingly euphemized discourses of the graduates of Harvard University. It remains, however, that the most hazy and fuzzy utterances of the latter open all doors in society whereas the most unpredictable linguistic inventions of the former remain totally devoid of value on the market of the school and in all social situations of the same nature.

There is a manner, ultimately quite comfortable, of "respecting the people" which amounts to confining them to what they are, in *pushing them further down*, as we could say, by converting deprivation and hardship into an elective choice. The cult of popular culture (whose historical paradigm is the *Proletkult*) is a form of essentialism, in the same way as the class racism which reduces popular practices to barbarism – of which it is often nothing more than the mere *inversion*, and a falsely radical one at that: indeed, it offers all the benefits of apparent subversion, of "radical chic," while at the same time leaving everything as it is, some with their actually cultured culture, capable of sustaining its own questioning, the others with their decisively and fictitiously rehabilitated culture. Populist aestheticism is yet another one of the effects, no doubt one of the most unexpected, of *scholastic bias* since it operates a tacit universalization of the scholastic point of view which is by no means accompanied by the will to universalize the conditions of possibility of this point of view.

Thus, we must acknowledge that if everything leads us to think that certain fundamental dispositions toward the world, certain fundamental modes of construction of reality (aesthetic, scientific, etc.), of *worldmaking*, constitute universal anthropological possibilities, these potentialities are actualized only in definite conditions and that these conditions, starting with *skholè*, as distance from necessity and urgency, and especially academic *skholè* and the whole accumulated product of prior *skholè* that it carries, are unevenly distributed across civilizations, from the Trobriand Islands to the United States of today, and within our own societies, across social classes or ethnic groups or, in a more rigorous language, across positions in social space. These are all very simple but very fundamental things, and it is not superfluous to insist on them, especially in a scholastic situation, that is, among people ready to join in the forgetting of the presuppositions inscribed in their common privilege. This simple observation leads us to an ethical or political program that is itself very simple: we can escape the alternative of populism and conservatism, two forms of essentialism which tend to consecrate the status quo, only by *working to universalize the conditions of access to universality.*

Logical Necessity and Social Constraints

To give a concrete and precise content to this kind of slogan, which at least has the virtue of being clear and rigorous, and to put us on notice against populist make-believe, we would need to reintroduce the whole analysis of the genesis of the specific structure of these quite peculiar social worlds where the universal is engendered and that I call fields. I believe indeed that there is a social history of reason, which is coextensive with the history of these social microcosms where the social conditions of the development of reason are engendered. Reason is historical through and through, which does not mean that it is on that account relative and reducible to history. The history of reason is the peculiar history of the genesis of these peculiar social universes which, having *skholè* as a prerequisite and scholastic distance from necessity (and from economic necessity in particular) and urgency as a foundation, offer conditions propitious to the development of a form of social exchange, of competition, even of struggle, which are indispensable for the development of certain anthropological potentialities.

If these universes are propitious to the development of reason, it is because, in order to make the most of yourself in them, you must make the most of reason; to triumph in them, you must make arguments, demonstrations, refutations triumph in them. To be recognized, that is, symbolically efficient in these universes, the "pathological motivations" about which Kant writes must be converted into logical motives. These social universes, which in some ways are like all other universes, with their powers, their monopolies, their egoisms, their interests, and so on, are in other ways very different, exceptional, if not a bit miraculous: in effect, the tacitly or explicitly imposed rules of competition in them are such that the most "pathological" functions are obliged to mold themselves into social forms and social formalisms, to submit themselves to regulated procedures and processes, notably in matters of discussion and confrontation, to obey standards that accord with what is seen, at each moment in history, as reason.

The scientific field, this scholastic universe where the most brutal constraints of the ordinary social world are bracketed, is the locus of the genesis of a new form of necessity or constraint or, if you will, of a specific legality, an *Eigengesetzlichkeit*: in it the logical constraints, whose specificity Bouveresse tried to uncover this morning, take the form of social constraints (and vice versa). Inscribed into minds in the form of dispositions acquired via the disciplines of the Scientific City (and, more simply, through the acquisition of state-of-the-art methods and knowledge), they are also inscribed in the objectivity of discussion, refutation, and regulated dialogue and especially, perhaps, in the form of positive and negative sanctions that the field, functioning as a market, inflicts upon individual products. At the extreme, each producer has no other clients than her competitors, who are thus her most merciless judges.

This is to say in passing that there is no need to wrench ourselves free from the embrace of relativism, to inscribe the universal structures of reason, no longer in consciousness but in language, by way of a revived form of the transcendental illusion. Jürgen Habermas stops his efforts in midcourse when he seeks in the social sciences a way out of the historicist circle to which the social sciences seem to condemn themselves (and in particular Grice's principles). There is no need to invoke a "beyond history" or to go along with the Platonic illusion which can be found, under different guises, in all fields, to account for the transcendence of (mathematical, artistic, scientific, etc.) works which are produced in scholarly fields and which are tested through the constraints or, better, the censorship, external or internal, that the field exerts on all those endowed with the dispositions it produces and demands ("Let no one enter . . ."). We must, by taking historicist reduction to its logical conclusion, seek the origins of reason not in a human "faculty," that is, a *nature*, but in the very history of these peculiar social microcosms in which agents struggle, in the name of the universal, for the legitimate monopoly over the universal.

A realist analysis of the functioning of fields of cultural production, far from leading to relativism, allows us to move past the alternative of antirationalist and antiscientific nihilism, on the one hand, and the moralism of the glorification of rational dialogue, on the other, toward a genuine *realpolitik of reason*. Indeed, I think that, short of believing in miracles, we can expect the progress of reason only from a political struggle rationally oriented toward defending and promoting the social conditions for the exercise of reason, a permanent mobilization of all cultural producers in order to defend, through continuous and modest interventions, the institutional bases of intellectual activity. Every project for the development of the human spirit which, forgetting the historical grounding of reason, depends on the sole force of reason and rational discourse to advance the causes of reason, and which does not appeal to political struggle aimed at endowing reason and freedom with the properly political instruments which are the precondition of their realization in history, remains prisoner of the scholastic illusion.

Notes

This text is Bourdieu's final address at the conference on "Geschmack, Strategien, praktiker Sinn" (Taste, Strategies and the Logic of Practice), held at the Free University of Berlin, October 23–4, 1989.

1 Alain V. Cicourel, "Habitus and the Development or Emergence of Practical Reasoning," also presented at the conference in the note above.
2 Jules Vuillemin, "Réflexion sur raison et jugement de goût," also presented at the conference.
3 Jacques Bouveresse, "La force de la règle," also presented at the conference.

A Paradoxical Foundation of Ethics

A possible point of departure for reflections on ethics is the existence of universally witnessed, metadiscursive or meta-practical, second-order strategies that agents employ in order to appear (in act or intention) to conform to a universal rule, even when their practice is at variance with perfect obedience to the rule or when it does not have perfect obedience to the rule as its principle. These strategies, through which one observes order notably by observing formalities, that is, by indicating recognition of the rule even in transgression, imply recognizing the fundamental law of the group: even if one does not respect the rule (the Kabyle are fond of saying that "every rule has its loophole"; and Marcel Mauss, "Taboos are there to be violated"), one must at least respect the fundamental law which demands that recognition of the rule be manifest. In a sense, from the group's point of view, there cannot be a more dutiful act than so-called "white lies" or "pious hypocrisies." If these deceptions that deceive no one are readily accepted by the group, it is because they contain an undeniable declaration of respect for the group's rule, that is, for the formal universal principle (universal since it applies to each group member) that is constitutive of the group's existence. These strategies of officialization, by which agents express their reverence for the official beliefs of the group, are strategies of universalization which accord the group what it demands above all else, that is, a public declaration of reverence for the group and for the self-representation it presents to others and to itself (as with the Kabyle father who presents a marriage between parallel cousins as if inspired by his respect for the rules of matrimony when in fact he is led by his concern with public disgrace or accepts it as a lesser evil; or the judge in a court of appeal who claims to have reached a decision based on deductions from legal principles, when his decision is really inspired or imposed by circumstantial considerations).

The (mental) representation the group has of itself can only be maintained through the incessant work of (theatrical) representation, through which agents produce and reproduce (albeit in and through mere fiction) at least the appearance of conformity to the group's ideal truth or ideal of truth. This work is imposed with a particular urgency upon those who act as the official spokespersons of the group. These persons, more than anyone else, cannot afford to be irreverent toward the collective ideal, in public or even in private. The group only fully accepts those who publicly show that they recognize the group. The sanctions of political scandal will inevitably befall the spokesperson who is disloyal, who does not really give the group what the group's recognition is worth to him.

Thus, groups always reward conduct that conforms universally (in reality, or at least in intention) to virtue. They particularly favor real or fictitious tribute to the ideal of disinterestedness, the subordination of the *I* to the *us*, or the sacrificing of individual interest to the general interest, which defines precisely the passage to the ethical order. Thus, it is a universal anthropological law that there are benefits (symbolic and sometimes material) in subjecting oneself to the universal, in projecting (at least) an appearance of virtue, and adhering externally to an official rule. In other words, the recognition that is universally accorded official rules assures that respect (formal or fictitious) for the rule brings about the profits of regularity (it is always easier and more comfortable to act according to rules), or "regularization" (in bureaucratic realism, the term "regularization of a situation" is sometimes used).

It follows that universalization (as an affirmation of the recognition of Plato's *koinon* – *common sense* – and *koinonein*) is the universal strategy of legitimation. Those who act according to the rule have the group on their side and at the same time ostensibly place themselves on the group's side through a public act of recognition of a communal norm, which is universal because it is universally approved within the limits of the group. They declare their agreement to conform to the group's point of view, valid for all potential agents, for a universal X. In opposition to the pure affirmation of subjective arbitrariness (because *I* want it or because that is the way *I* like it), the reference to the rule's universality represents increased symbolic power associated with its being put into form, into an official formula, into a general rule.

However, the existence of an interest in virtue and a profit in conformity to the social ideal of virtue are known universally, and no tradition is devoid of warnings against pharisaism, the ostentatious (and more or less hypocritical) defense of a "good cause" and virtuous exhibitionism. Universalization being the strategy of legitimation par excellence, a formally universal behavior can always be suspected of being the product of an effort to please or to gain the group's approval, of attempting to appropriate the symbolic force represented by *koinon*, the foundation of all choices presented as universal (*koinon*, or *common sense*, is what is just, both in the ethical, practical sense – as opposed to what is egotistical – and in the cognitive, theoretical sense – as opposed to what is subjective and partial). This is nowhere more true than in the political struggle for the monopoly of symbolic violence, for the right to say what is right, true, good, and to define all so-called universal values, where a reference to what is universally just can be the most important weapon.

But the disenchantment that a sociological analysis of the interest in disinterestedness may produce does not inevitably lead to a morality of pure intentions. Watchful only of usurpations of universality, this morality ignores the fact that the interest in, and the profit of, the universal are indisputably the most secure vehicle of progress toward the universal itself. With regard to the proverb, "hypocrisy is the homage paid by vice to virtue," we can focus on the negative and universally stigmatized concept of hypocrisy, or, in a more realistic manner, on the homage to virtue, universally recognized as a positive concept. And how can we ignore the fact that the critique of suspicion itself constitutes a kind of partaking in the profits of the universal? How can one fail to see that in its apparent nihilism, this critique does in fact encompass the recognition of universal logical or ethical principles, which it has to invoke, at least tacitly, in order to express or denounce the selfish, interested, partial, or subjective logic of strategies of universalization. Thus, while one may not object to the Aristotelian definition of man, humans may be considered irrational beings, even if their application of rational norms is judged sensible and reasonable. Similarly, one must not reproach the Hegelian model of state bureaucracy for ignoring the fact that those who serve the state also serve their own individual interest under the pretext of serving the universal, because one must tacitly admit that the bureaucracy can, as it pretends, serve the universal, and that the criteria and critiques of reason and morality can therefore be legitimately applied to it.

Kant's test of universalizability is the universal strategy of the rational critique of ethical claims (those who assert that others can be treated badly based on a particular property, for example skin color, can be questioned with regard to their own disposition to accept similar maltreatment if their skin were the same color). To state the question of the morality or the moralization of politics in sociologically realistic terms, we must consider in practical terms the conditions that would need to be fulfilled to keep political practices permanently subjected to a test of universalizability, so that the very workings of the political field force its actors into real universalization strategies. It would be a question of establishing social universes where, as in the Machiavellian ideal republic, agents had an interest in virtue, disinterestedness, and devotion to public service and the common good.

Political morality does not fall from heaven, and it is not innate to human nature. Only a realpolitik of reason and morality can contribute favorably to the institution of a universe where all agents and their acts would be subject – notably through critique – to a kind of permanent test of universalizability which is practically instituted in the very logic of the field. There is no more realistic political action (at least for intellectuals) than that which, giving political power to ethical critique, can contribute to the advent of political fields capable of favoring, through their very functioning, agents endowed with the most universal rational and ethical dispositions.

In short, morality has no chance of entering politics unless one works toward creating institutional means for a politics of morality. The official truth of the official, the cult of public service and of devotion to the common good, cannot resist the critique of suspicion that will endlessly uncover corruption, clientelism, ambitiousness, and at best a private interest in serving a public purpose. By a "legitimate imposture," in Austin's words, public persons are private persons socially legitimated and encouraged to think of themselves as public persons, thus to think of themselves and to present themselves as servants devoted to the common good. A politics of morality cannot but record this fact in catching public officials in the web of their own posturing, through the official definition of their official functions. Even more importantly, it is also among the tasks of a politics of morality to work incessantly toward unveiling hidden differences between official theory and actual practice, between the limelight and the backrooms of political life. This work of uncovering, disenchantment, or demystification, is anything but disenchanting. On the contrary, it can only be accomplished in the name of the same values of civil virtue (equality, fraternity, and especially disinterestedness and sincerity) with which the unveiled reality is at variance. And there is nothing discouraging, except perhaps for some "do-gooders," in the fact that those whose task it is to criticize, unveil, and hold accountable – journalists on constant lookout for scandals, intellectuals ready to fight for universal causes, lawyers wishing to defend and extend respect for the law, and researchers (like sociologists) eager to reveal concealed truths – will not be able to contribute to the creation of conditions for the institution of the rule of virtue unless the logic of their respective fields guarantees them the profits of the universal which are at the basis of their *libido virtutis*.

INDEX

Information to be found in the notes at the end of each chapter is signified by n after the page number.

Index by Ann Dean